Nature Praising God

Towards a Theology of
the Natural World

Dermot A. Lane

with a Foreword by Margaret Daly-Denton

LITURGICAL PRESS
ACADEMIC

Collegeville, Minnesota
www.litpress.org

1	2	3	4	5	6	7	8	9

Library of Congress Cataloging-in-Publication Data

Names: Lane, Dermot A., 1941- author. | Daly-Denton, Margaret, writer of foreword.

Title: Nature praising God : towards a theology of the natural world / Dermot A. Lane ; with a foreword by Margaret Daly-Denton.

Description: Collegeville, Minnesota : Liturgical Press Academic, 2023. | Includes bibliographical references and index. | Summary: "During the lockdown caused by the COVID crisis, streets were emptied, churches closed, and a relationship with nature developed in which new questions arose: Is God present in nature? Is communion with God in nature possible? Is there a relationship between the God of creation, the God of history, and the God we worship in Sunday liturgies? In Nature Praising God, Dermot Lane explores these questions by returning to the Bible. The result of these explorations is the outline of a new theology of nature praising God, with lessons for the way we worship God in our churches today"— Provided by publisher.

Identifiers: LCCN 2022046217 (print) | LCCN 2022046218 (ebook) | ISBN 9780814669105 (trade paperback) | ISBN 9780814669112 (epub) | ISBN 9780814669112 (pdf) | ISBN 9780814669129 (pdf)

Subjects: LCSH: Nature—Religious aspects—Christianity. | Ecotheology. | Nature in the Bible. | Bible—Criticism, interpretation, etc.

Classification: LCC BR115.N3 L36 2023 (print) | LCC BR115.N3 (ebook) | DDC 241/.691—dc23/eng/20221110

LC record available at https://lccn.loc.gov/2022046217

LC ebook record available at https://lccn.loc.gov/2022046218

CONTENTS

Chapter 5

Chapter 6

Chapter 7

ACKNOWLEDGEMENTS

THIS BOOK owes its origins to the lockdowns caused by the Covid-19 pandemic (2020–2022) in Ireland. During that time when churches were closed, people turned to nature to commune with the Creator God. There are many people in the background who made the publication of this book possible. In no particular order, I thank my long-time friend, Terry Tilley, Professor Emeritus of Theology, Fordham University, New York, who read the manuscript and offered, as always, constructive criticism.

I thank the professional staff of Messenger Publications: Director, Cecilia West, Carolanne Henry, Paula Nolan, Kate Kiernan, Fiona Biggs and Donal Neary SJ who gently kept alive the idea of a new book.

I'm grateful to the people of Balally Parish who have listened patiently to many of the ideas in this book in sermons and services, and were kind enough to offer helpful feedback.

Recently Father Jim Caffrey was appointed to Balally Parish. Jim is a man of many parts: a former student, a fellow diocesan priest, an outstanding youth leader in the Dublin diocese for sixteen years, parish priest of St Columba's, Iona Road, a Cistercian monk of five years' standing and now my teacher in the creative unity of contemplation and service, meditation and action, prayer and social engagement. For his friendship, support and encouragement in publishing this book I am most grateful.

A special word of thanks goes to my secretary Hazel Rooke. She is more than a secretary; she brought clarity and coherence to the gestation of the manuscript with great patience.

To all of the above, and others like the Balally Environment Group (BEG), the Laudato Si' Working Group (LSWG) of the Bishop's Conference, I offer my personal thanks.

FOREWORD

I WRITE these words in a déjà vu moment, when yet another dire warning has come from the United Nations: that it is now or never if our world is to avoid the worst impacts of the climate crisis. The UN set up its Intergovernmental Panel on Climate Change in 1988. The thirty-four years since then have seen considerable progress, but also much inertia. Sadly, the panel's sixth Assessment Report, just published, reflects what UN Secretary-General António Guterres calls 'a litany of broken climate promises'. Ireland remains a climate action laggard, with emissions still on a rising trajectory, and with pledged sustainable initiatives slow to materialise. We who claim the colour green should hang our heads in shame! Except that here in Ireland we can boast that there is a lively ferment of environmental awareness and action, particularly in faith communities. A prophetic leader, inspiring the Irish Church's growing ecological consciousness, is our own Dr Dermot Lane, an internationally recognised theologian who has been devoting his golden years to channelling a lifetime of theological learning into passionate advocacy for earth-care and climate justice. This he does in whatever time he has left after serving as a priest in Balally Parish for thirty years, where he ministered as a creative and far-sighted pastor for twenty-five years, utterly committed to the Second Vatican Council's vision for the Church.

The potential of the world's religious traditions to instil in their adherents an attentiveness to the earth that can spill over into a greater respect for it has long been recognised, even by many scientists. It has become painfully evident that graphs and statistics tend not to touch human hearts. But if people of faith can see the ecological crisis as a wake-up call to their religious and moral imagination, then powerful energies for restoration and renewal can be unleashed. And this is where the work of theologians comes in. The task of taking a new look at the Christian view of the natural world has, as Dermot explains, taken on a new urgency because of the climate crisis, the ongoing loss of biodiversity and the global pandemic. The challenge for theology today is to develop a new idiom that chimes with contemporary experience, culture and science. Far from being an esoteric scholarly pursuit, remote from everyday life, this quest has never been more pressing and more crucial for the future of our planet. It is a matter of helping today's followers of Jesus to move beyond the otherworldliness and dualism that distorted the theology they imbibed from childhood, enabling them to discover a new theology of nature in which earth-care is integral to Christian faith.

Following on from his 2020 book, *Theology and Ecology in Dialogue: The Wisdom of* Laudato Si', Dermot now argues for a retrieval of the forgotten, or at least underappreciated, biblical insight that nature praises God. This is a concept familiar from the Church's liturgy, where phrases such as 'All you have created rightly gives you praise' (Eucharistic Prayer 3) frequently occur. He brings his readers back to the biblical roots of the idea that nature praises God independently of human beings, drawing out its implications for eco-theological ethics and for Christian worship. This biblical tradition is a powerful antidote to the anthropocentric and instrumentalist view of nature that has allowed our planet to be ravaged. Dermot thinks outside the anthropocentric box to work out a fresh and theologically rich understanding of the natural world. This springs from his central intuition that attention to the capacity of nature to praise God will open us up to a new sense of our participation in a community of praise that embraces the entire earth. For Christians this involves recognising that the enlivening and rejuvenating Spirit of God is active in the whole creation and that this liveliness of the Spirit has been personified with the becoming flesh of the Word of God in Jesus and his sharing in the interconnectedness of the whole living community of earth.

Among the signs of hope for a healing of the damage we have done to our common earth home, Dermot mentions the 'turn to nature' that became evident over the last two years when church buildings were closed for public worship because of the Covid-19 pandemic. This has surely inspired people with a new sense of creation as an expression of the praise of God and an invitation to become part of that praise by 'giving voice to every creature under heaven' (Eucharistic Prayer 4). This can happen both through worship and through work to ensure the flourishing of all that God has created. Perhaps the recovery of a forgotten biblical insight has, as Dermot suggests, something to say to the much-needed reform of Christian worship in the twenty-first century. It will certainly give us a new understanding of what we mean and what we are committing ourselves to when we sing, 'Heaven and earth are full of your glory!'

Margaret Daly-Denton
6 April 2022

CHAPTER 1

Retrieving a Lost Conversation

Earth's crammed with heaven
And every common bush afire with God,
But only he who sees takes off his shoes;
the rest sit around and pluck blackberries.

(Elizabeth Barrett Browning, 1806–1861)

ANYONE FAMILIAR with the Hebrew Bible will notice that now and again different texts appear that portray nature praising God. This is particularly true of the Psalter, in which there is a fairly consistent theme of nature praising God.

a. A Sample of Texts on Nature Praising God

However, there are also other texts in the Bible with nature praising God. These include:

> Sing for joy, O heavens, and exult, O earth;
> break forth, O mountains, into singing!
> For the Lord has comforted his people
> and will have compassion on his suffering ones.
>   (Isaiah 49:13)

and

> The wilderness and the dry land shall be glad;
> the desert shall rejoice and blossom;
> like the crocus it shall blossom abundantly
> and rejoice with joy and shouting. (Isaiah 35:1–2)

Other examples in the Bible include: 1 Chronicles 16:31–33; Isaiah 40:10, 43:19 and 55:12; Philippians 2:10; Revelation 5:13.

The two exemplars from Isaiah above show that the praise of God takes place in the present and at other times in the future with the advent of the Messiah or the enthronement of the King.

The praise of God by the natural world is more evident in the Psalter. It is instructive to note that the last psalm in the Psalter concludes by saying: 'Let everything that breathes praise the Lord' (Psalm 150:6), as if to say, this is the purpose of the Psalter, a challenge not only for humans, but also for everything that breathes. The praise of God takes place on earth in his sanctuary (v. 1) and in the heavens (v. 1). This suggests a connection between earthly and heavenly praise of God.[1] All, in heaven and on earth, in the present and the future, are invited to join in the praise of God.

The best-known psalm in which everything that breathes praises God is Psalm 148. This psalm is largely post-Exilic and was probably recited in public worship (as was the first creation story in Genesis 1:1–28). The psalm has a number of striking features.

It begins and ends with the injunction 'Praise the Lord', addressed to all beings in the world. The word 'all' appears eight times and is addressed to all living creatures. Two broad categories are called to praise: the heavenly and the earthly. Within the earthly, you have humans alongside a long list of creatures from the natural world. The outreach of the invitation to praise God is comprehensive. The praise begins from above the earth:

---

1. John Endres, 'Psalm 150', in *The Paulist Biblical Commentary*, edited by J. Enrique Aquilar et al., Mahwah, NJ: Paulist Press, 2018, 520.

Praise him, sun and moon;
praise him, all you shining stars!
Praise him, you highest heavens
and you waters above the heavens! (Psalm 148:3–4)

Then it turns to the creatures on earth:

Praise the Lord from the earth,
you see monsters and all deeps,
fire and hail, snow and frost,
stormy wind fulfilling his command! (Psalm 148:7–8)

Next comes the human community:

Kings of the earth and all the peoples,
princes and all rulers of the earth!
Young men and women alike,
old and young together. (Psalm 148:11–2)

All of this praise is addressed to the Lord, 'for his name alone is exalted' (v. 13). The distinguished and highly respected UK scripture scholar Richard Bauckham describes this psalm as representing 'a cosmic choir of praise' or 'a symphony orchestra'.[2] John Endres notes that 'the psalmist avoids any sense of an exalted status for humans', preferring instead to focus 'on what they share in common, the call to worship'.[3] Both Bauckham and Endres point out that 'created beings praise God by being what they were created to be and fulfilling their own tasks and duties'.[4] For Bauckham, this praise of God by all creatures in Psalm 148 is:

the strongest antidote to anthropocentrism in the biblical and the Christian tradition.[5]

2. Richard Bauckham, *The Bible and Ecology: Rediscovering the Community of Creation*, London: DLT, 2010, 77 and 78.
3. John Endres, art. cit.
4. Ibid., 520, and Richard Bauckham, op. cit., 79.
5. Richard Bauckham, op. cit., 80.

In recognising this capacity of the natural world to sing praises, the psalmist is going beyond a purely instrumental view of nature. This call to join creation in praising God is not exclusive to Psalm 148. It can also be found in other psalms, such as Psalm 98:

> Make a joyful noise to the Lord, all the earth;
> break forth into joyous song and sing praises ...
> Let the sea roar and all that fills it,
> the world and those who live in it.
> Let the floods clap their hands;
> let the hills sing together for joy
> at the presence of the Lord ... (Psalm 98:4, 7–8)

Other examples exist outside the Psalter:

> Sing, O heavens, for the Lord has done it;
> shout, O depths of the earth;
> break forth into singing, O mountains,
> O forest and every tree in it! (Isaiah 44:23; similar texts can
> be found in Isaiah 55:12 and Joel 2:21–22)

This sample of texts emphasising nature's praise of God prompts a number of questions. What does it mean to say that nature praises God? How is it possible for the natural world to sing the praises of God? To modern ears, this sounds far-fetched. How can there be the praise of God without the exercise of free will?

There are several traditional answers to these questions, even if, in the end, they are unsatisfactory. The first suggestion is that nature inspires human beings to praise God. It is not nature in itself, therefore, that praises God, but human beings who praise God on behalf of nature. Nature functions as a prompt or a stimulus for the worship of God by human beings. This is clearly an anthropocentric response. It assumes that only human beings can praise God, even though we know that nature preceded the advent of the human.

A second explanation of these instances of nature-praising texts proposes that these texts are eschatological. Nature will praise God in the future by being part of the promised new heaven and the new earth. This response sidesteps the question of nature itself praising God and projects it into the future. In effect, nature praising God in the present is ruled out. Nature is seen in the future as a utilitarian or decorative add-on to the new creation. There is no recognition that nature in itself might be able to praise God in the present or that it might be part, in itself, in its own right, of the new creation.

A third suggestion replies that these nature-texts are merely metaphorical, or examples of poetic licence, or just forms of a rhetorical flourish that can arise out of the enthusiasm that sometimes accompanies intense experiences of the beauty of nature or mystical moments within prayer. This response seems to ignore the peculiar character of theological language. Theological language is, at its best, metaphorical, poetic, rhetorical and analogical. It is because of these literary devices that theology has insisted that every 'is' statement should be followed by an 'is not' statement. So, for instance, we might say that God is the creator of everything there is, but is not a 'thing' like other things. It is only in and through this dialectical relationship between what is and is not that we can get to know and experience the presence of God in this life. Thus some theologians see God as 'the ground of being', but not a particular being (Tillich). Without careful attention to this dynamic within theological language, we run the risk of reducing God to an object alongside other objects and ending up perilously close to idolatry. Acknowledgement of this peculiar character of theological language has been a constant within the Christian tradition. It can be found in Augustine (if you claim to understand God, then it is not God), in Aquinas (who insists on keeping the 'is' and 'is not' together), and the Council of the Lateran in 1215, which taught that there is no similarity between God and creatures without a greater dissimilarity. It is also worth noting that the great mystics brought together positive statements (*kataphatic*) and negative statements (*apophatic*) in their discourse about God. This emphasis has, over the centuries, given rise to a variety of theologies of symbolism, dialectic and analogy.

A fourth response to nature-praising psalms is to suggest that these are marginal and esoteric exceptions. However, before taking this stance, we should remember that a few similar texts can also be found in the New Testament in a saying of Jesus in Luke 19:40, in Revelation 4 and in Romans 8, which talks about creation groaning. In addition, some of the early Church Fathers echo the language of creatures other than human beings praising God, including Basil of Caesarea, who likens such praise to that of a chorus, and St John of the Cross, who saw such praise as a symphony.[6] Further, it should be noted that the idea of nature praising God can be found in a few places in the liturgy of the Catholic Church, for example in Eucharistic Prayer 3, which prays that:

> You are indeed holy, O Lord
> And all you have created rightly gives you praise.

Further, the Exultet in the Easter Vigil talks about the 'earth rejoicing' in the light of the resurrection. In addition, the dawn and midnight Masses for Christmas quote psalms praising God, such as

> Let the heavens be glad, and let the earth rejoice;
> let the sea roar and all that fills it;
> let the field exult and everything in it.
> Then shall all the trees of the forest sing for joy
> before the Lord, for he is coming,
> for he is coming to judge the earth. (Psalm 96:11–13)

Similar psalms appear in the Midnight Mass and the Mass during Christmas Day, such as Psalms 96:11–12 and 97:1–6.

What started out as a fairly straightforward examination of a few texts in the Bible portraying nature praising God has turned out to raise far more complex issues. Important questions arise about the capacity of the natural world in itself to praise God without taking refuge in an anthropocentric or a merely utilitarian view of nature. To guide us through some of the liturgical and theological complexities of these questions, we will outline the views of four scripture scholars who have dealt, in detail, with the significance of the nature-praising-texts of the Bible. But

---

6. Taken from Elizabeth A. Johnson, *Ask the Beasts: Darwin and the God of Love*, London: Bloomsbury Continuum, 2014, 276, who in turn refers in a footnote no. 17 to the work of James Schaefer, *Theological Foundations for Ecological Ethics*, Washington DC: Georgetown University Press, 2009.

before we consider what scripture scholars are saying about nature praising God, we should consider the significance of the personification of nature in the Bible.

b. A Note on the Personification of Nature

One way of opening up the discussion about nature praising God is to look at the personification of nature in the Hebrew Bible. Personification is about the attribution of human characteristics to the natural world, such as speaking, dancing and proclaiming. In the ancient world, personification was employed as a rhetorical device, designed to draw attention to neglected features of the world. As such, it is a linguistic convention that opens up the meaning of human experience and our encounter with the world around us. The personification of the natural world is found in literature and is by no means exclusive to the Bible.

From a theological point of view, the personification of nature in the biblical tradition is a multi-layered device. For example, what stands out in the Hebrew Bible with the personification of nature is the marked contrast to the deification of nature in surrounding cultures. In the neighbouring religions, nature or aspects of nature were often deified, especially among the polytheistic religions. For Israel, the personification of nature was a way of drawing attention to the supremacy of Yahweh over other nature-gods. One of the hallmarks of Jewish faith is the clear affirmation and strict adherence to the unity, oneness and sovereignty of Yahweh. Another dimension to the personification of nature is the way Israel highlights the capacity of nature to give praise and glory to the one God.

In some instances, the psalms present natural phenomena, such as the earth quaking (Psalm 99:1) and the sea roaring, and all that fills it, and the field exulting and everything in it (Psalm 96:11–12), as praising God. In other instances, you have nature singing, shouting and proclaiming the praises of God (Isaiah 42:10–12; 44:23; 49:13; 55:12). In some instances, the heavens, the earth and all that is in them are presented as praising God together (Jeremiah 51:48).

According to Hilary Marlow, the personification of nature in the Psalter operates at a number of different levels. It brings together nature and humans in praising God. Everything that has breath is called to praise the Lord (Psalm 150:6). This invitation to the whole of creation is spelt out in Psalm 148 which follows, more or less, the story of creation in the opening chapter of the Book of Genesis. At another level, the personification of nature highlights that the purpose of creation is to give glory to God. The whole of creation, not just humans, is invited to worship the one true God of Israel. A further function of the personification of nature is that it enables Israel to differentiate itself from the neighbouring cultures that had deified nature. In this way, the personification of nature 'de-deifies' nature, as it were. A fourth feature of the personification of nature is that it is a way, as already noted, of safeguarding the strict monotheism of Israel.[7]

In the light of these introductory remarks on the praise and personification of nature, we will now examine four different, but complementary, interpretations of the meaning of nature praising God.

---

7. See Hilary Marlow, 'The Hills are Alive! The Personification of Nature in the Psalter', in *Leshon Limmudim: Essays on the Language and Literature of the Hebrew Bible in Honour of A. A. Mackintosh*, edited by David A. Baer and Robert P. Gordon, New York, NY: Bloomsbury, 2013, 189–203, especially 190, 198, 199, 200.

CHAPTER 2

Biblical Commentators on
Nature Praising God

*We love (God), not only with our whole body, our whole heart,
and whole soul, but with our whole universe.*[1]

IT IS against the background of this introduction to texts that talk about
nature praising God and our brief account of the literary genre of personification that we can begin to ask the following questions. What does
it mean to say that nature praises God? How is it possible for nature to
praise God within the traditional mindset which assumes the existence
of freedom and consciousness when people praise the Creator? To be
more specific: How does the natural world of trees and flowers, of mountains and valleys, praise God? What kind of language are we using when
we talk about nature praising God? Is there any connection between
nature praising God and humans praising God in the liturgy, and if
there is a connection, then what is the difference between nature praising God and humans praising God? There is no simple answer to these
questions. There is, rather, a plurality of positions which, when examined, are more complementary than contradictory.

---

1. Pierre Teilhard de Chardin, *The Human Phenomenon*, Portland, OR: Sussex Academic Press,
1999, 213.

In the next couple of chapters, we will outline some answers to these questions. This discussion is still unfolding in biblical, theological and scientific circles. It has taken on a new urgency in the light of the climate crisis, in view of ongoing discussions about the nature of liturgy, declining attendances at liturgies, and in virtue of the 'turn to nature' during the Covid-19 pandemic when churches had to close down as public places of worship.

a. Terrence E. Fretheim's Pioneering Contribution

In 1987, US scripture scholar Terence E. Fretheim published a groundbreaking article on 'Nature's praise of God in the Psalms'.[2] Fretheim uncovers some fifty references to nature praising God, appearing in twenty-five different contexts, with fourteen in the Psalms.[3] He gives special attention to Psalm 148, as do most commentators. In that psalm, as already seen, the sun and the moon and the stars, the highest heaven, sea monsters, fire and hail, snow and frost, mountains and hills, fruit trees, wild animals and cattle, creeping things and birds are invited to praise God (Psalm 148:3–10).

Fretheim outlines some background presuppositions behind these different texts that portray nature praising God. To appreciate this background, readers need to move from an anthropocentric view of reality to a more inclusive one, one that recognises the intrinsic value of the non-human world alongside the human. Further, the outlook in the ancient biblical world saw the natural world as 'alive' and having 'a certain inwardness and interiority' that made relationships possible within creation.[4] In saying this, Fretheim is quick to point out that 'this does not necessarily lead to pan-psychism or vitalism (the notion that rocks and animals somehow have a degree of consciousness) but rather suggests a greater continuity between the animate and the inanimate worlds than moderns

---

2. In *Ex auditu*, 3, 1987, 16–30. This article was subsequently incorporated as a chapter in his book *God and the World in the Old Testament: A Relational Theology of Creation*, Nashville, TN: Abingdon Press, 2015, 249–68.
3. Here we will follow the article as published in *God and the World in the Old Testament*, ibid., 249.
4. Ibid., 255.

have commonly been willing to claim'.[5] A third principle, noted by Fretheim, is that 'God is not only a God of history; but is also a God of Nature'.[6] A fourth presupposition is that a certain 'symbiosis of the human and non-human'[7] is found in the praise of God, a point we will take up later on. It is against the background of these principles that Fretheim is able to make sense, not only of nature praising God, but also of the close relationship that exists between humans and non-humans in giving praise to God.

Many of these praising texts are invitations to nature to praise God so as to bring out the glory of God in the present simply by being themselves. Other texts have an eschatological orientation on two levels. Some of the texts look towards the enthronement of God as King in the future (Psalm 96:11–12 and Psalm 98). Other texts point to nature being part of the new heaven and the new earth to come. In a detailed chart, Fretheim shows how most of the fifty texts praising God are hymns.

b. Richard Bauckham's Distinctive Vision

Following on from Fretheim, an equally significant contribution to the theme of nature praising God can be found in the work of Richard Bauckham.[8]

Bauckham claims, like Fretheim, that creation's praise of God 'is the strongest antidote to anthropocentrism in the biblical and Christian tradition'.[9] He further emphasises the need for humanity to move out of a domination model to that of a living community of creation model, in which close collaboration between God, humanity and other creatures takes place. For Bauckham, creation's praise of God reminds us 'that all creatures bring glory to God simply by being themselves and fulfilling

---

5. Ibid.
6. Ibid., 261, 264.
7. Ibid., 264.
8. See Richard Bauckham, 'Joining Creation's Praise of God', in *Eco Theology: A Christian Conversation*, edited by Kiara A. Jorgenson and Alan G. Padgett, Grand Rapids, MI: WB Eerdmans, 2020, 7, 45–59; *The Bible and Ecology: Rediscovering the Community of Creation*, London: DLT, 2010, especially Chapter 3; and 'Being Human in the Community of Creation', 15–47.
9. Richard Bauckham, *The Bible and Ecology*, ibid., 80; he repeats this in his 2020 article, ibid., 43.

their God-given role in God's creation'.[10] In support of his position that all creatures give praise to God by being themselves, he quotes Daniel Hardy and David Ford who argue that 'creation's praise is not an extra, an addition to what it is, but the shining of its being, the overflowing significance it has in pointing to the Creator simply by being itself'.[11] Further, 'to recognise creation's praise is to abandon an instrumental view of nature. All creatures exist for God's glory', and 'when we learn to see the non-human creatures in that way, we glimpse their value for God has nothing to do with their usefulness to us'.[12] For Bauckham, creation's praise of God stands out as a critique of a purely instrumental view of nature and the common perception of nature as something to be used solely for the needs of human beings. Further, according to Bauckham, the biblical theme of the worship that all creation offers to God is:

> The most profound and life-changing way in which we can recover our place in the world as creatures, alongside our fellow creatures.[13]

In his commentary on Psalm 148, which he takes as the most extensive example in the Hebrew Bible of creation's praise of God, he describes this psalm as a 'cosmic choir of praise' in which 'more than thirty categories of creatures are addressed'.[14] There is a strong emphasis on the word 'all' scattered throughout the psalm, and as such it occurs eight times in the psalm. Elsewhere, he says 'a more appropriate analogy would be a symphony orchestra'[15] made up of different mutually complementary parts from within the community of creation.

In brief, for Bauckham, the psalmist in 148 is putting before us a certain reciprocity between the different parts of our praise of God: 'other creatures help us to worship, while we add to their worship by drawing

---

10. Richard Bauckham, 'Joining Creation's Praise of God', art. cit., 47.
11. Daniel Hardy and David Ford, *Jubilate: Theology in Praise*, London: DLT, 1984, 82.
12. Richard Bauckham, 'Joining Creation's Praise of God', art. cit., 49.
13. Richard Bauckham, *The Bible and Ecology*, op. cit., 76.
14. Ibid., 77.
15. Ibid., 78.

it into our worship'.[16] In listening to nature's invitation to praise God, we are inspired as human beings to worship the Creator of all, and we come to realise that humans and other creatures together can worship God more effectively in following their underlying vocation.

Bauckham's suggestion that nature praises God 'simply by being itself' is not shared by everyone. There is, of course, an element, an important element, of truth in this claim, but it needs qualification. Not everything that nature is or does, praises God. There are positive and negative sides to nature. There is pain and suffering in nature which surely does not praise God and, for many, this reality of pain and suffering within nature is a serious obstacle to human faith in God, not to mention the possibility of nature praising God. Further, it must be noted that talk about nature praising God raises the obvious question – what do we mean by nature? Are we talking about nature in the past, or nature in the present or nature in the future? It is increasingly evident that nature in the present is less and less capable of praising God because of its mindless exploitation by the industrial and technological revolutions. Yet it must be admitted that, despite this insensitive exploitation of the natural world, there are moments in the seasons of the years that nature praises the Creator and inspires humans to join in praising God.

c. David G. Horrell's Constructive Critique

David G. Horrell is the third participant in this exploration of the meaning of nature praising God. Horrell appreciates the important contribution of Bauckham to this debate, but nevertheless raises questions for Bauckham. For example, he is unhappy with Bauckham's suggestion that nature praises God simply by being itself. He points out that 'none of the biblical texts, in the psalms and elsewhere, quite say that creation actually worships God just by being itself'.[17] At the same time, Horrell does acknowledge that many of the praising psalms witness to the greatness and wonders of creation, and thereby point to the greatness and

---

16. Ibid., 82.
17. David. G. Horrell, *The Bible and the Environment: Towards a Critical Ecological Biblical Theology*, New York, NY: Routledge, 2010, 85.

praiseworthiness of God.[18] A good example of this can be found in Psalm 19:

> The heavens are telling the glory of God; and the firmament proclaims his handiwork. (Psalm 19:1, ESV)

Horrell cites other psalms that catalogue the wonders of God's creation, such as Psalms 136 and 104. He is making a fine distinction between creation as witness to God's greatness, and creation's praise. However, is there not a very close relationship between the wonder of creation and the worship of God, especially in the context of the Hebrew Bible, where creation is the basis of the praise and worship of God?[19]

In spite of Horrell's reservations about nature praising God as expressed in 2010 in his *The Bible and the Environment*, one year later he comes around to qualifying this reservation by acknowledging that 'creation *does* already praise God but in ways that are partial and inadequate, marred not only by human activity but also by the ongoing suffering in which creation and humanity remain enmeshed'.[20] There are a number of points worth underlining here. Horrell agrees that creation does already praise God, but only in a limited way, limited by human activity, that is by the ongoing domination and exploitation of nature by individual governments and multinational corporations. It is increasingly evident that the capacity of creation to praise the Creator is being trampled upon and damaged on a daily basis in virtue of so much interference with the integrity of creation. In this context, Horrell asks an important question: 'What actions will most foster the ability of creation to express its praise?'[21] In response to his own question, he emphasises the importance

---

18. Ibid., 50.
19. See Dermot A. Lane, 'Ecology and Liturgy' and '*Laudato Si*' and the Cosmic Eucharist', in *Theology and Ecology in Dialogue*, Dublin: Messenger Publications, 2020/New York, NY: Paulist Press, 2021: 115–32 and 133–52.
20. David G. Horrell and Dominic Coad, "The stones would cry out' (Luke 19:40): A Lukan contribution to a hermeneutics of creation's praise', in Scottish Journal of Theology, 64 (1), 2011, 29–44.
21. David G. Horrell and Dominic Coad, "The stones would cry out' (Luke 19:40): A Lukan contribution to a hermeneutics of creation's praise', in Scottish Journal of Theology, 64 (1), 2011, 29–44, at 43.

of promoting beauty within creation as a way of enhancing creation's praise of God. In cultivating beauty within creation, he suggests the adoption of 'non-utilitarian, non-economic, and non-anthropocentric criteria'[22] to achieve this goal.

In the light of Horrell's reservation about nature praising God by being itself, he goes on to offer another interpretation of nature praising God. He notes that many of these texts have an eschatological orientation (Psalms 96:11–12; 98:7–9; 150:6; Isaiah 42:10; 44:23; Joel 2:21–22). These texts point to a future in which nature and humans together will flourish and praise God. For example, the enthronement psalms point to a time when the king is enthroned and all, nature and humans, will praise God as King. Other texts point to the promise of a new heaven and a new earth (Isaiah 65:17–25), a vision of the future that influences conduct in the present. Horrell makes a compelling case to go beyond a view of nature praising God simply in the present to a view of nature and humans praising God in the future. If we can see nature as a constituent in the new heaven and the new earth, then this particular eschatological perspective gives a basis, at least an ethical basis, for respecting nature in the present and overcoming a purely instrumental view of nature. In this view, an eschatological outlook on nature praising God provides a foundation for the adoption of a theologically informed ecological ethic in the present.

Another difficulty that Horrell has with Bauckham should be noted. He wishes to introduce what he calls a 'critical and constructive' approach to the interpretation of the Bible and, in particular, to the texts that point to nature praising God. According to Horrell, Bauckham fails to recognise the influence of the ecological crisis upon his approach to the Bible. Further, says Horrell, greater recognition should be given to the fact that many texts in the Bible are ambiguous, and this should also be taken into account when interpreting the Bible on these questions. The influence of our contemporary context should not be underestimated in approaching the Bible. This particular question cannot be addressed here, since our primary concern is about making sense of those texts which present nature as praising God, except to note that there is no neutral point of view. All humans are immersed socially, culturally and historically in the world

---

22. Ibid., 43.

around them and cannot avoid their particular locations as they read and comment on the biblical text.

Part of Horrell's distinctive contribution to this debate is his emphasis on the eschatological orientation of nature praising God, and the significance of this for the development of ecological ethics. Also significant is his call for the application of a critical and constructive hermeneutic to biblical texts and the need for this engagement to include a doctrinal lens in approaching the Bible. In addition to this, Horrell does talk about creation's cry of praise of God which, he says, stands out as a 'rebuke of humanity's acquisitive self-absorption'.[23] Horrell is also concerned about the failure of humanity to relate to non-human creation in ways informed by peace and justice, and sees this as a kind of rebuke that could contribute to the notion of ecological sin.

A further point worth noting is, that by emphasising the role of eschatology, Horrell is reminding us that creation is itself an unfinished project and this points to a future, a future in which humanity and creation together will praise and glorify God. If creation, in the future, will participate in the eternal praise of God in the new creation, then this has deeply ethical consequences for the way we treat nature in the present.

A final point is that Horrell is critical of Bauckham insofar as he fails to take an adequately informed hermeneutical approach to the biblical text, and thereby gives the impression that it is just a matter of rediscovering what is already in the texts. This fails to take account of the ambiguity of biblical texts, such as Genesis 1:28–31, and drives home the need to adopt a more critical and constructive engagement with biblical texts, one conscious of the interpreter's location, as noted above. Horrell wants to go beyond a rediscovery model in approaching the biblical texts. It is not simply a matter of reading what is already there in the Bible, as if certain biblical texts had somehow been neglected. For Horrell, Bauckham gives the impression that we can step outside our contemporary contexts and interests. This approach, says Horrell, ignores the ambiguity and multivalency of the biblical texts.[24]

---

23. David G. Horrell, *The Bible and the Environment*, op. cit., 134.
24. David G. Horrell, 'Ecological Hermeneutics: Reflections on Methods and Prospects for the Future', available at http://hdl.handle.net/10571/16642. Deposited in Open Research, Exeter, 1 April 2015, University of Exeter, UK.

To sum up, Horrell is critical of Bauckham's approach to the Bible, which gives the impression that all that is required is to rediscover what is already in it. Horrell wants to highlight the influence of the contemporary context in reading the Bible today. To do this, Horrell says we must adopt a 'critical and constructive approach': critical in terms of acknowledging the ambiguity of some texts, and constructive in terms of reading the Bible through the lens of our contemporary context and some faith commitment.

d. Mark Harris's Call for a New Theology of Nature

Mark Harris takes careful account of the contributions made by Fretheim, Bauckham and Horrell. He seeks to build on their insights, sometimes by incorporating them into his theology of nature praising God and, at other times, offering a constructive critique of them. Harris is a distinguished scientist, as well as a scripture scholar, so he keeps a weather eye out for what scientists might be saying about nature.

Harris differs from his colleagues by calling consistently for what he refers to as a 'robust theology of nature' as a way forward.[25] This means developing a theology of nature that is separate and distinct from an anthropocentric theology of creation. The standard theologies of creation have been developed at the expense of an explicit theology of nature. He formulates the question he is asking in the following way: 'Is there any sense in which non-human creation might be able to praise the Creator in and of itself?', and not, therefore, in dependence upon humans.[26]

According to Harris, there are two different ways of approaching what it might mean to say that nature praises God. One is to say that we are dealing with metaphorical accounts of the human praise of God and that such metaphorical accounts are a human response to the wonders of

---

25. Mark Harris, "The trees of the field should clap their hands' (Isaiah 51:12): What does it mean to say a tree praises God?', in *Knowing Creation: Perspectives from Theology, Philosophy and Science*, edited by Andrew B. Torrance and Thomas H. McCall, Grand Rapids, MI: Zondervan: 2018, 287–304, at 291, 288, 299 and 301.

26. See Mark Harris, "Let the floods clap their hands, let the hills sing together for joy' (Psalm 98:8): Is joy the theological and emotional shaper of the inanimate world?', paper delivered to the European Society for the Study of Science and Theology, Assisi, 2014, 1–8, at 2 and 7. Article available online as a PDF. Accessed 10 August 2021.

creation. This is the approach most people would take and is the easiest to understand.

Harris, however, wants to explore a different approach. He suggests we should try to take a more literal approach and seek to imagine how mountains and trees in and of themselves could be said to praise God. The first approach, namely that the texts are metaphorical expressions of the human praise of God, is too anthropocentric and too anthropomorphic. In other words, human praise is too much to the fore, and nature is simply in second place in the background. This distinctive outline of two different approaches to the question helps us to appreciate the radical character of what is involved in working out what Harris calls a new, robust theology of nature. Harris does not pretend to offer a worked-out theology of nature, but he does seek to point towards a new way forward for concentrating on nature without denying the importance of the human.

To that end he outlines a number of 'building blocks' for the construction of a theology of nature. These building blocks include the following points. There is a need to work out a theology of the relationship that exists 'between non-human creatures and the Creator'.[27] This means taking account of recent evolutionary theologies of creation which highlight the immanent presence of God within every creature and not just humans.

A further building block is the challenge to describe the relationship between non-human creatures and the Creator, 'independently of humans',[28] even though we can only approach this question from a human perspective. Another building block for a theology of nature is the recognition that the themes of salvation and judgement (eschatology) must be taken into account because they are present in the biblical texts of nature praising God. Examples of the eschatological completion of nature can be found in the Psalms (especially 96:11–13; 98:8–9) and Isaiah (35:1; 44:23). With Horrell, Harris emphasises the importance of eschatology as intrinsic to any theology of nature praising God. Some psalms have a

---

27. Ibid., 7.
28. Ibid., 7. This notion can take account of the evolution of human beings from non-human nature and place humanity within nature praising God rather than placing the human as so unique in creation as to be practically unnatural.

vision of nature as part of the promised new heaven and the new earth, and this affects how we see nature in the present. This point was also emphasised by Horrell, who suggested that eschatology is something not only of concern for humans, but of significance for nature. A fourth building block for any theology of nature praising God must also be able to take account of nature's groaning and suffering in the present.

The value of these building blocks is that they force the reader to work out a theology of nature that is not anthropocentric or utilitarian or anthropomorphic. Instead, these building blocks nudge us to move into a new direction, into another framework, into a different paradigm for approaching a theology of nature. This new paradigm posits the immanence of God in the whole of creation, and opens the way for developing a theologically informed spirituality of nature, a point that will be taken up presently. These shifts invite us to work out a theology of nature that is no longer reliant on an anthropocentric theology of creation. This new location for a theology of nature is colourfully described by Harris as an uncharted 'no-man's-land' or, as he says, a 'no-anthropocentrist's-land', between theology and anthropology, without reverting to a traditional theological anthropology.[29]

Harris's framing of the question forces us to go beyond the modern assumption that the praise of God can only be given by human beings who are alive, free and self-conscious, and that these qualities are not present in a modern understanding of the natural world. Harris is challenging theology to think outside the anthropocentric box of the modern mindset, and to come up with a non-anthropocentric theology of nature. In favour of what Harris is proposing, it should be noted that there is a view that the natural world can praise God, as expressed in the Psalms and Isaiah. This view is present in the Book of Revelation in the New Testament (4:7–11; 5:13), and is found in the writings of some of the early fathers (e.g. Tertullian and Theodore of Mopsuestia) and Hildegard of Bingen, as well as in the Canticle of St Francis.

This call by Harris for a new theology of nature is all the more significant in the light of a recent UN Environment Programme report, *Making Peace with Nature* (18 February 2021). Commenting on the report,

---

29. Ibid., 7. Accessed 28 April 2021.

UN Secretary-General António Guterres pointed out that 'humanity is waging a senseless and suicidal war on nature, that is causing human suffering and enormous economic losses while accelerating the destruction of life on earth'. In his Introduction to the report, Guterres makes a number of significant suggestions. He highlights the need:

- to re-evaluate … our relationship with nature;
- to see nature as an ally that will help us achieve the sustainable development goals;
- to protect and restore nature;
- to create a world at peace with nature.[30]

This EU Report on *Making Peace with Nature* was followed up in June 2022 with a proposed legal document entitled *EU Nature Restoration Regulation* published by the Institute for European Environmental Policy. This document proposes a new legislative framework aimed at the restoration of the integrity of nature for member states of the EU.

The neglect and mindless exploitation of nature over the centuries has been a key contributor to the ever increasing loss of biodiversity. There is now a new awareness of the social and psychological health benefits attached to the restoration of nature.[31]

To gather up these biblical voices, we can say that Fretheim and Bauckham emphasise that nature praises God by being itself. Horrell and Harris are at one in highlighting the eschatological character of some nature texts that praise God. There are of course differences in detail among the four interpreters of the biblical witness, and we will comment on these after hearing some theological voices on the meaning of nature praising God.

30. United Nations Environment Programme, *Making Peace with Nature: A scientific blueprint to tackle the climate, biodiversity and pollution emergencies*, Report, 18 February 2021, https://www.unep.org/resources/making-peace-nature, accessed 14 August 2021.
31. Institute for European Environmental Policy, *The proposed EU Nature Restoration Regulation: The path to nature's recovery*, 22 June 2022, https://ieep.eu/publications/the-proposed-eu-nature-restoration-regulation-the-path-to-nature-s-recovery, accessed on 29 June 2022.

CHAPTER 3

Theological Commentators on Nature Praising God

It is a kind of theological folly to suppose that God has made the entire world just for human beings, or to suppose that God is interested in only one of the millions of species that inhabit God's good earth.[1]

UNTIL FAIRLY recently, most of the debate about nature praising God was biblically based. A number of scripture scholars, largely from the Reformed tradition, have gathered the data, analysed it, and pointed to the presence of a plurality of positions on the meaning to be attached to nature praising God. This work requires equally careful theological engagement. To initiate that engagement, we will outline in broad strokes some Catholic voices on this debate. We will look briefly at the contribution of different voices and move from there to examine what light *Laudato Si': On Care for our Common Home* (2015) might shed on this increasingly important subject, especially in view of the ecological crisis, the increasing loss of biodiversity, the Covid-19 pandemic, and the 2021 UN report *Making Peace with Nature*.

---

1. Desmond Tutu, Foreword to *Global Guide to Animal Protection*, edited by Andrew Linzey, Champaign, IL: University of Illinois Press, 2014.

On 12 June 2021, the G7 meeting in Cornwall issued a similar call 'to protect nature' as part of their response to the climate emergency. This call by the UN and the G7 'to protect nature' highlights the urgency for theology to engage creatively not only with the biblical data about nature but also with the new evidence coming from scientists on the damage being done to nature by our modern habits of mindless extraction, production and consumption, without due regard to the integrity of nature and the importance of some form of sustainability going forward into the future. The construction of a new non-anthropocentric theology of the natural world has never been more urgent in the history of humanity than just now.

a. Thomas Berry

Tom Berry, a Passionist priest who describes himself as a 'geologian', does not address explicitly the meaning of nature praising God. He does, however, provide important background material that will help towards an understanding of why it is possible for nature to praise God. Berry is very insistent that, at this critical time, humanity needs a new story in which we can locate the natural world in its relationality and dependency on the larger universe story informed by the new cosmologies. In that context, Berry talks about a cosmic liturgy.[2] Within this cosmic liturgy, rituals were established to put humans in touch with the changes of the cosmos: dawn and dusk, the daily sequence of sunlight and darkness, the increase and decline in the phases of the moon, the winter solstice … the periods of dark descent; and then comes the rise into a world of warmth and light and the blossoming of plants.[3] These changes are described by Berry as 'moments of grace, moments when the sacred world communicated itself with special clarity to the world of humans'.[4] It is within this larger liturgy taking place in the universe that Berry would locate nature's capacity to praise God. The cosmic praise of the

---

2. See Thomas Berry, 'The Universe as Cosmic Liturgy', in *Selected Writings on the Earth Community*, selected with an Introduction by Mary Evelyn Tucker and John Grim, New York, NY: Orbis Books, 2014, 52–62.

3. Ibid., 53

4. Ibid.

Creator in the rhythms of life and death informs nature's praise of God. As Berry points out:

> From an early period, Christians adopted a liturgy that carefully observed the correspondences of human praise with the numinous moments of dawn and sunset and with the transitions of the various seasons of the year.[5]

Mary Evelyn Tucker and John Grim, in their Introduction to Berry's *Selected Writings on the Earth Community*, note that, for Berry, 'the seasonal cycles of birth, death and re-birth', put Christians in touch with the movement within the Christian liturgy 'from Christmas to Good Friday to Easter'.[6] Berry is acutely aware that we 'are changing the chemistry of the planet … disturbing the bio systems, altering the geological structures and the functioning of the planet', and that this is having a damaging effect on the natural world, by closing down life systems and turning the planet into 'an earth waste land'.[7] The more species we lose, the more we diminish different modes of the divine presence. This, in turn, is giving rise to a loss of intimacy with creation and a disconnectedness from the natural world, all of which make it more difficult to understand the meaning of nature praising God. It is because of our loss of intimacy with creation and our increasing disconnectedness from the natural world that modern people find it difficult to understand the possibility and meaning of nature praising God.

The value of Berry's reflections is that he enlarges the context in which we can begin to make sense of nature praising God. He does this by connecting nature's praise of God with the wider cosmic liturgy taking place over millions and millions of years. In effect, he links nature's capacity to praise God as found in the biblical texts with roots in our contemporary understanding of the world we inhabit today. For Berry, the larger cosmic liturgy exists within the community of creation and, as

---

5. Thomas Berry, *The Great Work: A Way into the Future*, New York, NY: Random House, 1999, 23–24.

6. In Thomas Berry, *Selected Writings on the Earth Community*, op. cit., 49.

7. 'Religions awaken to the Universe', in *Selected Writings on the Earth Community*, op. cit., 70.

such, inspires and sustains the living community of creation in its praise of God.

b. Elizabeth A. Johnson

Another theologian who has made, and is making a distinctive contribution to the subject of nature praising God is Elizabeth A. Johnson.[8] The first point to note about Johnson's short treatment of nature praising God is that she also locates this subject within the larger context of the community of creation, in contrast to the domination of creation model. Clearly, there is little room for nature praising God within the domination model. Within the context of the domination model, nature is seen as created for modern man to exploit. In contrast, in the living community of creation, the human exists within the community of creation, not above or below creation, but as part of God's creation. Clearly, there is as little room for nature praising God within the domination model as there is for slaves praising their appointed taskmasters.

Johnson begins her reflection on nature praising God, or as she calls it, creation praising God, with Psalm 104, to illustrate how the whole community of creation has a sense of wonder at the abundance and the giftedness of creation which inspires praise and gratitude. She notes, like Berry, that the rhythm of day and night, the marking of the seasons by the moon and the sun, are a gift from God.

She then goes on to explore Psalm 148, in which she finds a large array of creatures praising God. And why? Because God 'commanded and they were created' (Psalm 148:5). She notes how the sky, the sea and the land are part of a grateful community of creation giving praise to God in their own distinctive ways. Like other commentators, she likens this community of praise to that of 'a cosmic choir' or 'a symphony orchestra', each like a member of an orchestra playing their own distinctive part. These metaphors are taken from patristic and medieval sources.[9]

---

8. Johnson addresses this question in *Ask the Beasts: Darwin and the God of Love*, New York, NY: Bloomsbury, 2014, in a section entitled 'Creation's Praise and Lament', 273–80. She also takes up this question in 'Animals' Praise of God', in *Interpretation: A Journal of Bible and Theology*, 2019, 73, 259–71.

9. In this regard, Johnson refers to the work of James Schaefer, *Theological Foundations for Ecological Ethics*, Washington DC: Georgetown University Press, 2009, 103–20.

In answer to the question, how can all these creatures praise God, she replies:

> By virtue of being created, of being held in existence by the loving power of the Creator Spirit, all beings give glory to God simply by being themselves.[10]

In this context, she quotes Richard Bauckham's comment that 'a tree does not need to do anything specific in order to praise God'.[11]

There are two important theological points in this quotation that should be highlighted. The first is the importance of a theological doctrine of creation. It is because all creatures are created by God that they can praise God. Further, it is because all creatures are 'held in existence by the loving power of the Creator Spirit'[12] that they can praise God. The doctrine of creation and the theology of the Spirit poured out on 'all flesh' are essential to understanding nature praising God, points that we will take up presently and later in Chapter 6.

Johnson has no difficulty in acknowledging that nature's praise of God is a poetic metaphor. Such metaphors 'have cognitive as well as aesthetic value'.[13] Without the metaphor of nature praising God, we humans could overlook or forget about the presence of God in our world. Nature praising God, therefore, reminds us that 'we are all fellow creatures of the same life-giving God ... sharing the world given as gift by God'.[14] The invitation of the psalmists to other creatures to sing, to be glad, to rejoice and to shout does not initiate their praise. Instead, creation is already praising God, with or without human attention, and the praising-psalms bring this to human awareness. Along with others, Johnson notes that some psalms have an eschatological orientation, anticipating the new heaven and the new earth. She refers to the Book of Revelation (5:13) to illustrate that in the end of time all creatures, all voices, will join together in giving praise to God. This united praise of God reminds humans that

---

10. Elizabeth A. Johnson, *Ask the Beasts*, op. cit., 276.
11. Ibid., 277. The quotation from Bauckham is found in *The Bible and Ecology*, op. cit., 79.
12. Ibid., 276.
13. Ibid., 277.
14. Ibid.

nature has value in itself and that this particular value is not based on nature's usefulness to humanity.

c. *Laudato Si'*: On Care for Our Common Home

Laudato Si' was written in 2015, well after the biblical debate on the meaning of nature praising God sparked by the groundbreaking article by Terence Fretheim. *Laudato Si'* also came after the significant theological contributions of Tom Berry and Elizabeth Johnson. The encyclical addresses the ecological crisis from a variety of points of view: biblical, spiritual, theological, ethical, liturgical, economic and environmental. It is not in any sense a systematic treatment of the ecological crisis, but does draw on a variety of disciplines. It adopts the principle or methodology of 'integral theology', which seeks to integrate the many insights of different disciplines into a coherent whole.

It is of significance for our theme of nature praising God to note that *Laudato Si'* is presented within a framework of prayer. It opens with the prayer '*Laudato Si'*, *Mi Signore*', 'Praise be to You, My Lord', taken from the Canticle of St Francis of Assisi.[15] The encyclical concludes with two prayers at the end, one for all who believe in God and the other for Christians. Both prayers are theologically rich. And it could be said that the mood of the encyclical is prayerful. The Christian Prayer is entitled 'A Christian prayer in union with creation', and it begins: 'Father, we praise you with all creatures'.[16] At the introduction of *Laudato Si'* to the world, Cardinal Peter Turkson, Prefect of the Dicastery for Integral Human Development, and regarded as the chief architect of *Laudato Si'*, emphasises that the underlying attitude of *Laudato Si'* is one of 'prayerful contemplation'.[17]

Laudato Si' begins by admiring how St Francis of Assisi, having gazed at the sun, the moon, the smallest of animals, would 'burst into song drawing all creatures into his praise'[18] of God. The encyclical notes

---

15. *Laudato Si'*, 1.
16. Ibid., 246.
17. Peter Turkson, 'Official Presentation of *Laudato Si'*', Rome, 18 June 2015, available at: https://pres.vatican.va/content/salastampa/it/bolletino/publico/2015/06/18/0480/01050 .html#eng.
18. *Laudato Si'*, 11.

how St Francis 'communed with all creation, even preaching to the flowers, inviting them to praise the Lord, just as if they were endowed with reason'.[19] *Laudato Si'* laments the disappearance of plants and animal species due to human activities. Because of this interference, it regrets that 'thousands of species will no longer give glory to God by their very existence nor convey their message to us'.[20]

Further on, the encyclical explicitly returns to the theme of nature praising God, noting how the Psalms 'also invite other creatures to join us in this praise' of God the Creator.[21] And the reason why other creatures can praise God is that God 'commanded and they were created (Psalm 148:3–5)'.[22] In other words, the idea of nature praising God is grounded in a theology of creation. As we will see in Chapter 7, this theology of creation should include reference to creation out of nothing, the gift of continuous creation, and the promise of a new creation. If we forget or ignore or jettison such a theology of creation, then the idea of the possibility of nature praising God will not make much sense.

This understanding of the reasons for nature praising God is confirmed in the observation in *Laudato Si'* that 'when we can see God reflected in all that exists, our hearts are moved to praise the Lord for all His creatures and to worship Him in union with them'.[23] In other words, the idea of nature praising God will not make any sense unless it is grounded in a clear theology of God as creator of heaven and earth. Creation comes from God and returns to God in the act of praise. Thus, the theology of nature praising God is premised on a theology of creation.

At the centre of this theology of creation is an understanding of creation as gift in *Laudato Si'*. In a number of places, the encyclical refers to creation as gift. In doing so, it makes a distinction between creation and nature: 'the word "creation" has a broader meaning than "nature" … creation is about God's loving plan in which every creature has its own value and significance'.[24] In contrast 'nature is usually seen as a system which can

19. Ibid.
20. Ibid., 33.
21. Ibid., 72.
22. Ibid.
23. Ibid., 87.
24. Ibid., 76.

be studied, understood and controlled, whereas creation can only be understood as gift from the outstretched hand of the Father' ... and 'as a reality illuminated by the love which calls us together into a universal communion'.[25] It is important to note the emphasis here on creation as a gift, and that this gift is illuminated by the love that calls humanity into a universal communion.

Elsewhere, *Laudato Si'* points out that 'the gift of the earth with all its fruits belongs to everyone',[26] that 'the land is not a commodity, but rather a gift from God',[27] and that 'acceptance of our bodies as God's gift is vital for welcoming and accepting the world as a gift from the Father'.[28] It is this awareness of the earth, of the land and its food as gift that 'strengthens our feeling of gratitude for the gift of creation'.[29]

There is a theology of creation as gift in *Laudato Si'* awaiting further development. UK theologian Simon Oliver points us in the right direction for this development. He argues persuasively that for 'a gift to be truly gift, it must be received and acknowledged as such', otherwise it becomes a commodity, something useful and forgotten tomorrow.[30] According to Oliver, 'to understand creation as gift is to realise that all existence and life, precisely as gift, is called to thankfulness'.[31] It is the commodification of nature by modern culture that blinds us to nature praising God. However, once the intrinsic value of nature is accepted, and once its beauty is recognised, we can begin to make sense of nature praising God as found in the Hebrew Bible.

This theme of nature praising God is peppered throughout *Laudato Si'* and reaches a high point in the last chapter, where a rich theology of the Eucharist is condensed into a few paragraphs.[32] On the one hand

---

25. Ibid.
26. Ibid., 71.
27. Ibid., 146.
28. Ibid., 155.
29. Ibid., 227.
30. Simon Oliver, 'Every Good and Perfect Gift is from Above: Creation *ex nihilo* before Nature and Culture', in *Knowing Creation: Perspectives from Theology, Philosophy and Science*, op. cit., 39.
31. Ibid., 44.
32. *Laudato Si'*, 235–37. For an elaboration of the significance of the Eucharist in this context, see Dermot A. Lane, *Theology and Ecology in Dialogue: The Wisdom of Laudato Si'*, Dublin: Messenger Publications, 2020, 139–46.

Laudato Si' says, 'through our worship of God we are invited to embrace the world on a different plane. Water, oil, fire and colour are taken up in all their symbolic power and incorporated into our act of praise'.[33] In other words, through these sacramental symbols, nature participates in our praise of God. On the other hand, it is 'in the Eucharist … all that has been created finds its greatest exultation … the world which came forth from God's hands returns to Him in blessed and undivided adoration'.[34] Once again, a connection is made between the theology of creation and the praise of God.

In relation to the debate about creatures praising God by being themselves, *Laudato Si'* recognises that other creatures can give glory to God. In this context, *Laudato Si'* draws on two sources. One is the *Catechism of the Catholic Church*, which says 'by their mere existence they bless Him and give Him glory'.[35] The other source is the German bishops, who 'speak of the priority of being over that of being useful'.[36]

To sum up this outline of *Laudato Si'* on nature praising God, the following points stand out. Chief among these is the need to link nature praising God with a strong theology of creation. This should be followed by a theology of creation as gift and promise. A third point is the importance of recognising the sacramental character of creation, which will be discussed in Chapter 4.

d. A Retrospective on This Debate

It may be helpful at this stage to give a retrospective glance at these biblical and theological voices on the meaning of nature praising God. Fretheim and Bauckham have helpfully emphasised that nature praises God by being itself, and fulfilling its God-given role in the world. However, it must be recognised that due to the negative impact of the industrial and technological revolutions, nature itself is less and less able to be itself and that, therefore, it is less obvious to the observer that nature is praising God, or indeed will be able to praise God in the

---

33. *Laudato Si'*, 235.
34. Ibid., 238.
35. See *Catechism of the Catholic Church*, no. 2416, which is quoted in *Laudato Si'*, 69.
36. See *Laudato Si'*, 69.

future because of the degree to which it has been exploited, dominated and instrumentalised.

One must be grateful to Horrell, Harris and Johnson for introducing eschatology into this discussion about nature praising God. It is not enough, however, to say that there are texts in the Psalms and in Isaiah that are eschatological. Before these texts can credibly be categorised as eschatological, they must have some foothold in present experiences, otherwise we are in danger of promoting a new opium of religion. What is this foothold in experience that enables us to hope that nature, along with other humans, will be part of the new creation and the new earth?

Could it be the experience of beauty, even terrible beauty, in nature that animates such hope? Could it be the order, the complex structure (the *Logos*) and wisdom (*sapientia*) of the natural world, that portends a future? Could it be the creativity that is intrinsic to the survival of the natural world? Could it be the rhythm of life and death and rebirth that seems to be at the centre of the natural world? Could it be that the dynamism of such activities is in itself a form of nature praising God, an expression of nature praising God in the present which also, at the same time, intimates a promise in the future? Could it be that where there is life in nature, there is also the co-presence of the Spirit of God indwelling in nature, that this Spirit is the source of beauty, creativity and order, and that, therefore, it is the Creator Spirit that inspires and animates nature's praise? Could it be that defilement, sterility and disorder mark the ways in which the Creator-Spirit's inspiration and animation have been suffocated? In this way, there is a pneumatological platform for a new theology of the natural world, a theme that will be developed in Chapter 5.

There are, of course, hazards in making these suggestions about the Spirit, especially the dangers of animism, pan-psychism and pantheism. Firstly, a strong theology of creation that recognises the breath of God poured out on creation from the beginning can avoid these kind of pitfalls. Secondly, this strong theology of creation would have to include different dimensions to creation, such as creation out of nothing, the gift of ongoing creation, and the promise of a new creation – points we will take up in Chapter 7. Thirdly, such a theology of creation would have to be informed by the Christ-event, especially the impact of the death and resurrection of Christ on the rest of creation.

Mark Harris calls for the development of a robust theology of nature. He has encouraged us to think outside the anthropocentric box. What is needed, therefore, in this non-anthropocentric theology of nature? One way of responding to this challenge would be to look more closely at the possibilities of a theology of grace as an intrinsic part of nature. This would require not only the development of a Spirit-centred theology of creation but also the possibility of exploring a graced naturalism, that is, an understanding of nature as graced from the beginning of time.[37]

It should be noted that others have also issued a similar call for a new theology of nature. For example, John McCarthy and Nancy Tuchman have outlined a programme that seeks to address the disenchantment of the universe, the desacralisation of creation, and the mechanisation of nature. They have called for a new discourse around nature, a discourse of depth that overcomes the dualisms of the natural and the supernatural, spirit and matter, body and soul.[38] These particular dualisms have arisen out of a loss of any sense of divine immanence within creation. Further, these dualisms would need to be overcome in any new theology of nature. Chapter 4 will outline what a non-anthropocentric theology of nature might look like.

---

37. Roger Haight, among others, develops a grace-filled naturalism in *Faith and Evolution: A Grace-Filled Naturalism*, New York, NY: Orbis Books, 2019, especially 198 and 221.
38. John McCarthy and Nancy C. Tuchman, 'How We Speak of Nature: A Plea for a Discourse of Depth', in *Heythrop Journal*, LIX, 2018, 944–58.

CHAPTER 4

Towards a New Narrative about Nature

Hope is never dead
until this bewildered earth
stops throwing up roses.[1]

THE PURPOSE of this chapter is to outline a number of small, preliminary steps towards the construction of a non-anthropocentric theology of nature. This chapter will be followed by two specific chapters which will deal respectively with pneumatological and Christological aspects of a non-anthropocentric theology of nature.

a. Nature as a Living Community

The first step in developing a non-anthropocentric theology of nature is to move out of a human-centred model of creation into a recognition of creation as a living community. Whatever about the original intention and meaning of the divine command to 'fill the earth and subdue it; have dominion over the fish of the sea … ' (Genesis 1:28), the reception of these verses in the modern era became detached from the original intention of the divine command, and this has been detrimental to the life and integrity of the natural world. In turn, this modern reception has

---

1. 'Flowers know nothing of our Grief', in Moya Cannon, *Donegal Tarantella*, Manchester: Carcanet Press, 2019.

given rise to a licence to exploit the natural world for the exclusive use of human beings. There has been a damaging shift from dominion to domination, akin to a political shift from a commonwealth to a power-grab, with negative consequences for nature, especially in the areas of climate change, the loss of biodiversity, and the Covid-19 crisis. Many theologians have been critical of the damage done to the natural world in the name of dominion, and have moved towards the construction of a community of creation model.[2] It should be stated that this turn to the natural world as a living community is not about reducing everything to the lowest common denominator; instead, it is about recognising that everything has a unique place and a role to play within the wider community of creation. There are, of course, mutually enriching differences and diversities within the community of creation. These differences are not absolute, but relational, and find their origin and unity in the plan of God. The community of creation is a radically theocentric community, in contrast to the domination model, which has been predominantly anthropocentric. The uniqueness of human and non-human beings within the community of creation derives from their relationships within the plan of God. This community of creation recognises and respects the essential role that nature plays within the larger universe.

The community of creation model is inspired by Psalm 24:1: 'The earth is the Lord's and all that is in it, the world and those who live in it'. This vision of the living community of creation includes all that makes up our universe: the birds and the bees, the trees and the mountains, creatures and humans, and the invisible world that makes the visible world possible. This living community of creation is manifested in the interconnectedness and relationality of everything in the world. Within this model, humans are not above other creatures, but alongside other creatures, not separated from other creatures but fellow creatures, not outside nature but inside nature. This community of creation is held together by the Spirit of God poured out at the dawn of time on all reality. The Spirit of God suffuses the whole of creation from the beginning of time to the present, and into the future with the promise of a

---

2. This can be found in the work of Elizabeth A. Johnson, Denis Edwards, Richard Bauckham, Seán McDonagh, Celia Deane-Drummond and Daniel Horan, to mention just a few.

new community of creation. The Spirit of God inhabits the natural world, as well as the human world, in a variety of different ways and in varying degrees.

Laudato Si' distances itself explicitly from the interpretation of dominion as domination. It acknowledges that 'We Christians have at times incorrectly interpreted the scriptures'[3] in this regard, and goes on to say: 'We are called to recognise that other living beings have value of their own in God's eyes'.[4] Consequently, the encyclical points out that: 'In our time the church does not simply state that other creatures are completely subordinate to the good of human beings as if they had no worth in themselves and can be treated as we wish'.[5] Instead, other creatures have intrinsic value independent of their usefulness[6] because each creature 'is an object of God's love'[7] and, therefore, 'reflects in its own way a ray of God's infinite wisdom and goodness'.[8] Consistent with this view that all are precious in the eyes of God, *Laudato Si'* affirms that human beings 'are part of nature, included in it and thus in constant interaction with it'.[9] In effect, the human is not above or below nature, but exists as 'part of nature' and 'in nature'. Nature is alive through the energy of the Holy Spirit poured out 'in the beginning', and it is supported through the interconnectedness of all living creatures within God's creation.

Then, as if to drive home this point about the value of the natural world, *Laudato Si'* expands the vision to point out: 'Eternal life will be a shared experience of awe, in which each creature, resplendently transfigured, will take its rightful place and have something to give to those poor men and women who will have been liberated once and for all'.[10] In highlighting the intrinsic value of the natural world, *Laudato Si'* is drawing on the unity that exists between creation and eschatology, between shared origins and shared destiny. For some, this may not go far enough, but

---

3. *Laudato Si'*, 67.
4. Ibid., 69.
5. Ibid.
6. Ibid., 140; see also 33 and 69.
7. Ibid., 77.
8. Ibid., 69.
9. Ibid., 139.
10. Ibid., 243.

for others it reflects, in contemporary language, some of the implications of the biblically based understanding of the whole community of creation. In this way, *Laudato Si'* is sowing the seeds of a more robust, non-anthropocentric theology of nature.

b. Nature as Grace-Filled

A second step in developing a preliminary theology of the natural world must be to address the question of grace. Nature is endowed with the grace of the Spirit of God. We live in a grace-filled universe. This large claim is grounded in a theology of the immanence of the Spirit of God poured out on all creation. The Spirit of God is described in the Hebrew Scriptures as present 'in the beginning', not only in the Book of Genesis (2:7 and 1:1–2), but also in the Psalms (36:6; 104:1–14), the Book of Job (12:10, 27:3 and 34:14–15) and Ezekiel (37:1–14).

The history of the relationship between nature and grace is multi-layered. There have been different emphases on grace down through the centuries from Augustine (uncreated grace), to Aquinas (created grace), to the Reformation (grace alone), to Karl Rahner's distinctive contribution in the twentieth century to a unified theology of grace summed up in what he called 'the supernatural existential', meaning that every human being is graced with a fundamental orientation towards God. All would agree that grace is about the gift of the Spirit of God to every human being and that this gift is unearned and unmerited. In the twenty-first century that gift of the spirit of God is perceived to embrace the whole of creation alongside every human being. In this sense we live in a world that is graced by the presence of the spirit of God. If sacraments are vehicles of divine grace, then creation is rightly recognised as a sacrament. The history of grace up to the twentieth century was played out within the confines of an anthropocentric theology of grace and did not have within its purview a contemporary recognition of the possibility of a non-anthropocentric theology of the natural world.

In the twenty-first century it is increasingly evident that the Spirit of God dwells in creation and is active not only in human lives, but also in the lives of other creatures and in the life of the earth (Psalm 33:6). It is worth noting in this regard that *Laudato Si'* points out that 'The life of the Spirit is not dissociated from the body or from nature or worldly realities'.[11] Rather the Spirit is present as embodied in the natural world, in human beings, in other creatures, and in the affairs of the world. Nature, the whole of nature, is graced by the Spirit of God from the beginning of time and throughout time into the future. Roger Haight, along with others, has developed a theology of a grace-filled nature.[12] This gift of grace is an expression of the love of God: it suffuses all reality, it holds the existence of creation in being, and it accompanies all of life. This grace is about the immanent presence of God in the world, in and through the gifts of the Spirit and the Word. The universal grace of God, present throughout creation, evokes wonder and gratitude, which leads to a response of prayer and worship.

In other words, the theology of grace, until very recently, was developed within an anthropocentric paradigm. This modern anthropocentrism operated out of a mechanistic, graceless understanding of the natural world. The natural world was not perceived as a place of grace. This outlook on the natural world as a domain devoid of grace is the subject of critique by a number of theologians. For example, Dan Horan points to the existence of an 'anthropocentric privilege that has had the effect of excluding the non-human world as part of the image of God and thereby granting a licence to humans for dominion over non-human creation'.[13] David G. Kirchoffer challenges theology today to overcome the presence of 'an egotistic anthropocentric'[14] understanding of existence which has diminished our appreciation of the natural world. Neil Ormerod and Christina Vanin talk about the existence of a 'hyper anthropological culture (which is) cut off from cosmological meaning and values' and so removed 'from the rhythms and cycles of nature'. The net effect of this is

---

11. Ibid., 216.
12. See Roger Haight, *Faith and Evolution: A Grace-Filled Naturalism*, New York, NY: Orbis Books, 2019, especially Chapter 4.
13. Dan Horan, 'Deconstructing Anthropocentric Privilege: *Imago Dei* and Non-human Agency', in *The Heythrop Journal*, 60, 2019, 560–70, at 560–61.
14. David G. Kirchoffer, 'How Ecology Can Save the Life of Theology: A Philosophical Contribution on the Engagement of Ecology and Theology', in *Theology and Ecology across the Disciplines: On Care for Our Common Home*, edited by Celia Deane-Drummond and Rebecca Artinian-Kaiser, London: T&T Clark, 2018, 53–63, at 57.

that 'the natural world is seen as simply a point of extraction (mining and agribusiness) and a site for dumping our waste'.[15] This anthropocentric paradigm has resulted in a number of damaging dualisms, unsympathetic to a theology of the natural world: nature and grace, Spirit and matter, body and soul, materialism and mysticism, sacred and secular. As noted above it ignores the beauty, creativity and order in the world and defiles, sterilises and fouls the natural world.

To overcome these dualisms, we invoke by contrast Karl Rahner's theology of grace. This theology of grace has had an overarching influence on the whole of Rahner's theology, and is of particular significance for understanding a theology of the relationship between nature and grace today. For Rahner, the grace of God in the world is informed by two related but indivisible moments. On the one hand, we have what Rahner calls God's gracious self-communication to the world or, as he puts it at times, God's self-bestowal on everything in the world. This action of God takes place from the dawn of time and is, therefore, present and active in the world from the beginning, and not as a once-off but as a continuous, divine presence in the world. On the other hand, this action of God in the world affects the interiority, the very constitution of creation and humanity. This reality of God's self-communication brings about a particular disposition and orientation within everything in the world. Rahner calls the effect of this divine presence in the world the gift of self-transcendence. Everything in the universe has an underlying orientation towards self-transcendence. This allows Rahner to talk about the graced self-transcendence of material creation in the natural world and in the world of human beings. The self-bestowal of God on the world, given in the act of creation, brings about an inner dynamism of self-transcendence throughout the universe, not just in human beings, but in the whole of material creation.[16]

From the very beginning matter is graced with the gift of self-transcendence. There is no matter without grace, no grace without matter,

---

15. Neil Ormerod and Christina Vanin, 'Ecological Conversion: What Does it Mean?', in *Theological Studies*, vol. 77 (2), 2016, 328–52, at 341–42.

16. Karl Rahner, *Foundations of Christian Faith: An Introduction to the Idea of Christianity*, London: Darton Longman & Todd, 1978, Chapters 2 and 3.

no gift of the Spirit without matter, no matter without the Spirit.[17] It is this gracious presence of God in the world that enables transitions from matter to life, and from biological life to the emergence of conscious, self-reflective human beings. These particular shifts are the result of the ongoing presence of the endowment of creation *ab initio* with the gift and dynamism of self-transcendence. This gift of self-transcendence is made possible by the ongoing, enduring, gracious self-communication of God to the world through creation and its historical manifestation in the Christ-event.

One powerful but neglected expression of this omnipresence of the grace of God in the world can be found in the Christian doctrine of 'creation out of nothing', a doctrine that is more than just an account of the world's origins, but also includes the ongoing presence of God's grace holding everything together and contains an implicit promise of a new creation. We will return to this theme of 'creation out of nothing' in Chapter 7.

To begin to see nature as graced, we must move out of a static universe into a world that is open, dynamic and relational. Within this world, grace is not some kind of add-on to creation, but rather something that is interior and constitutive of creation itself. The grace of God is not some 'thing', but is the dynamic *relationship* that exists between God and the world and the world and God, a relationship that holds everything in existence. The grace of God is the enduring presence of God that began 'in the beginning' with the outpouring of the Spirit which continuously holds everything together, from nothing to something, from non-being to being, from non-existence to the gift of life. It is this grace of God that enables a dynamic movement from matter to living creatures and from living creatures to self-conscious human beings. This means we must see the natural world not simply in terms of being, but also in terms of becoming, not simply as static but also as processive, not only in terms of what is, but also in terms of what is yet to be. This dynamic outlook on the natural world accords with the revelation and promise of the new creation 'in Christ' (2 Corinthians 5:17; Romans 8:18–23; Revelation 21:1–5).

---

17. I am grateful to Terrence W. Tilley for this succinct formulation of the relationship between grace and matter.

In emphasising the presence of the grace of God in the natural world, we must not forget the darker side of nature, summed up in words by Alfred Lord Tennyson (1809–1892) that 'Nature is red in tooth and claw'. On the one hand the natural world evokes a sense of awe and wonder, especially in terms of the cooperation, beauty and interconnectedness of everything in the world. On the other hand, however, nature is suffused with competition, suffering and violence, a subject that is too vast and important to address in this small volume. Nonetheless, any theology of nature must remind itself of the fiercely negative and dark dimensions of nature, which are not to be confused with treating nature as a point of extraction. These disturbing dimensions of nature seem to be more evident than ever before in the known history of the universe. Without this corrective one's theology of nature will appear to be too idealistic and romantic. In approaching this conundrum of life, account should be taken of the resonance that exists between life, death and rebirth within the cycle of nature and the unity that obtains within the Paschal mystery of the historical life, death and resurrection of Jesus as the Christ.

To conclude this brief outline of nature as graced, it must be noted that we Christians see the community of creation which includes the natural world as ordered to Christ, the one who personally represents God's invitational outreach to creation and, at the same time, as creation's fullest response to that grace-filled invitation. This is a point that will be developed further in Chapter 6.

c. Nature as a Book

A third step in moving towards a non-anthropocentric theology of nature is to see nature as a book, to be read and interpreted. This approach is also found in Augustine, Aquinas, Bonaventure and the Franciscan tradition. In our time, *Laudato Si'* points out that: 'God has written a ... book whose letters are the multitude of created things present in the world'.[18] Nature as a book, and therefore as a text, does not interpret itself. It is like any other text, open to different interpretations; in the biblical tradition alone, many interpretations of the natural world are present. Indeed,

---

18. *Laudato Si'*, 85. Other references to nature as a book can be found scattered throughout *Laudato Si'*, at 6, 12 and 239.

the text of nature is itself deeply ambiguous, at times evoking awe and wonder and, at other times, inflicting fear and pain and suffering.

In reading the book of nature in the twenty-first century, we have at our disposal resources that were never available before: magnified microscopes, telescopes and nano-technology. Through the findings of the sciences, especially the new cosmologies, quantum physics and biological evolution, we can discover things about nature that were never seen before in the modern era. Modern science opens up new vistas and new questions about the natural world, requiring careful scrutiny and interpretation, as well as a constructive critique of biblical texts (see the discussion of David G. Horrell in Chapter 2).

This understanding of nature as a book is not new; it has been present in the Judeo-Christian tradition. A good example can be found in Saul, the Jew, drawing on his Jewish theology of creation, and Paul, the Christian, influenced by the Christ event. Paul writes:

> Ever since the creation of the world, his eternal power and divine nature, invisible though they are, have been understood and seen through the things he has made. (Romans 1:20)

In the life of the early church, and in the Middle Ages, nature was seen as a resource for learning more about human existence and about the place of humans in the natural order, and the relationship between creation and the creator. In a well-known quotation, Augustine suggests:

> Some people, in order to discover God, read a book. But there is a great book: the very appearance of created things. Look above and below, note, read. God whom you want to discover did not make the letters with ink; He put in front of your eyes the very things that He made. Can you ask for a louder voice than that?[19]

Within these different traditions it was not just idle curiosity but a deep appreciation 'that nature was a resource for learning about humanity and

---

19. Augustine, *The City of God*, Book 16, and *Sermons*, 68.6.

its place in the cosmic hierarchy'.[20] In this regard, we need only think for a moment about how much nature has taught humanity about medical science, about the caring and healing of the whole community of creation. However, in the light of the ambiguous character of nature, and the incompleteness of nature, it is necessary to recover and interpret the book of nature alongside the book of the Bible. Nature is a work in progress, not a finished project.

d. Nature as Sacramental

Against this background of nature as a living community, as grace-filled and as a book to be interpreted, we can now begin to see some of the theological reasons for describing nature as sacramental. Nature is theocentric in virtue of the outpouring of the Spirit and the Word of God 'in the beginning', and the deep embrace of 'all flesh' in history through the Incarnation.

This sense of the natural world as sacramental has its roots in the Hebrew Bible. As already noted, Judaism has a strong, foundational theology of the natural world. For Jews, the universe is alive with the presence of the Spirit of God, especially in the light of the Spirit's activity as seen in Genesis and the Psalms. For Jews, the natural world is described by a number of different metaphors: the 'throne of God',[21] the 'sanctuary of God', and a 'cosmic temple'.[22] Given the liturgical orientation of the different theologies of creation in the Bible, especially in the Psalms and Genesis, creation assumes what we today would call a sacramental quality, embodying a divine presence throughout the whole community of creation. This outline is reflected in the sacramental liturgy of the tent, the tabernacle and the temple. A fundamental spiritual and sacramental presence permeates Judaism and Christianity. If we do not sense, indeed experience, the presence of the Spirit in creation, it is unlikely that we

---

20. Simon Oliver, *Creation: A Guide for the Perplexed*, London: Bloomsbury T&T Clark, 2017, 101.

21. See Isaiah 6:1.

22. See William P. Brown, *The Seven Pillars of Creation: The Bible, Science and the Ecology of Wonder*, New York, NY: Oxford University Press, 2010, 37; and Jon Levenson, *Creation and the Persistence of Evil: the Jewish Drama of Divine Omnipotence*, New York, NY: Harper & Row, 1988, 86.

will be able to encounter God in the liturgy of the temple, or in the liturgy of the Christian churches. As UK theologian Simon Oliver sums up: 'If God is to be met in the temple made by hands, this is only because God is first met in the temple of divine making, namely creation itself'.[23]

It is noteworthy that during the Covid-19 lockdown, when churches were closed, some people communed instinctively with the universal presence of God in the natural world, and this became especially evident in visits to gardens, forests and mountaintops. The Covid-19 crisis made some aware that the material world is imbued with a deep spiritual presence. The natural world is itself the primordial sacrament of the universal presence of God around us. *Laudato Si'*, quoting patriarch Bartholomew, says:

> Christians are called to accept the world as a sacrament of communion.[24]

The encyclical develops this emphasis on communion with nature in various ways. It talks about a 'sublime communion',[25] which 'fills us with a sacred, affectionate and humble respect'.[26] It also refers to the presence of a 'deep communion with the rest of nature',[27] and a 'universal communion as existing throughout the natural world'.[28] One way of grasping this emphasis on communion can be found in a principle formulated by Thomas Berry:

> The universe is not a collection of objects but a communion of subjects.[29]

Further, this symbolic and sacramental outlook within *Laudato Si'* enables us to talk about nature as 'a continuing revelation of the divine',[30] as 'a

---

23. Simon Oliver, op. cit., 18.
24. *Laudato Si'*, 9.
25. Ibid., 89.
26. Ibid.
27. Ibid., 91.
28. Ibid., 88.
29. Thomas Berry, *The Great Work: Our Way into the Future*, New York, NY: Random House, 1999, 82.
30. *Laudato Si'*, 85.

locus of God's presence',[31] as 'the dwelling place of the Spirit of life'[32] and as 'nothing other than a certain kind of art, namely God's art impressed upon things'.[33] *Laudato Si'* continues: 'The Spirit of life dwells in every living creature and calls us to enter into a relationship with him'.[34] This 'contemplation of creation allows us to discover in each thing the teaching God wishes to hand on to us'.[35]

This vision of nature as sacramental is grounded in the Incarnation of the Word of God in the flesh of Jesus. As Matthew T. Eggemeier points out, summarising von Balthasar: 'The Incarnation expresses in concentrated form the sacramental world view of the Christian tradition in which creation is the very medium through which God is revealed'.[36] The importance of the Incarnation will be discussed further in Chapter 6. The ultimate foundation for this understanding of nature as a living community, graced and sacramental, is twofold: the theology of creation and the doctrine of Incarnation which, though distinct, are inseparable, constituting the one divine action of God's gracious self-communication to the world in different phases.

---

31. Ibid.
32. Ibid., 88.
33. Ibid., 80.
34. Ibid., 88; see also 80 and 238.
35. Ibid., 85.
36. Matthew T. Eggemeier, 'A Sacramental Vision: Environmental Degradation and the Aesthetics of Creation', in *Modern Theology*, 29, July 2013, 338–60, at 352.

CHAPTER 5

A Nature-Based Pneumatology

THE BELGIAN poet Catherine de Vinck notes how time seems simply to go on and on and:

> *Yet the gifting never ceases:*
> *Nests filled with eggs, fields swell with edible plants, water*
> *continues to rise out of the deep, hidden wells*
> *pulled by the moon, see waves un-scroll themselves*
> *forming on the beach.*
> *What disappears returns defying decay and death*
> *In a corner of the yard a simple tulip blooms year after year*
> *Naming itself red and new in the spring air.*[1]

The purpose of this chapter is not to work out a fully fledged pneumatology.[2] Instead, it seeks to introduce pneumatology in so far as it sheds some light on a theology of nature. This purpose deliberately restricts the scope of this chapter.

How might the concerns of Mark Wallace, John McCarthy, Mark Harris, the UN Environment Programme (2021) and others to build a

---

1. Catherine de Vinck, 'Gifting', The Forum on Religion and Ecology at Yale, online newsletter, May 2019, accessed 24 March 2020.

2. Pneumatology is the study of the spirit (*pneuma*) in the world.

non-anthropocentric theology of nature be met? There is a need to construct a robust theology of nature, especially in the light of climate change, the ongoing loss of biodiversity, and questions about the meaning of nature praising God.

One possibility might be the development of a religious naturalism. This is a scientific understanding of the natural world that evokes religious impulses. A good example of this can be found in a book by Ursula Goodenough entitled *The Sacred Depth of Nature*. The 'goal of this book' is 'to present an accessible account of a scientific understanding of nature and then suggest ways that this account can call forth appealing and abiding religious responses'.[3] Goodenough's book, which is scientifically informed in terms of cosmology and evolution, will not be sufficiently theological for some, though in fairness it does not claim to be theological. It is a most stimulating book and a highly respected account of origins and evolution within the scientific community, and it paves the way for a theology of nature, opening up new avenues for dialogue between religion and science.

Another way of answering the opening question of this chapter is to explore the possibility of developing a nature-based pneumatology, that is a theology of the Spirit that takes account of the beauty, creativity and complexity of nature which is compatible with a scientific understanding of nature. There has been little enough formal dialogue on the relationship between the Spirit and nature, with some notable exceptions to this generalisation, such as Elizabeth Johnson, Denis Edwards, Rosemary Radford Ruether, Sally McFague, Celia Deane-Drummond, Daniel Castelo and others. This neglect of the relationship between the Spirit and nature has had negative consequences for our understanding of nature as well as for our understanding of the Spirit in the modern era.

a. Neglect of the Spirit
A good point of departure is to note the relative neglect of the Spirit within western theology. The Spirit is often referred to as the forgotten person of the Trinity, the Cinderella of theology, and one of the most

---

3. Ursula Goodenough, *The Sacred Depth of Nature*, New York, NY: Oxford University Press, 1998, xvii.

misunderstood doctrines of contemporary theology. These difficulties are compounded by a number of dualisms within traditional theology, such as spirit and matter, grace and nature, creation and redemption, between a Jewish theology of the Spirit and a Christian theology of the Spirit. These dualisms have, unwittingly, given rise to distorted views of the presence and action of the Spirit in the world. For example, the Spirit is often seen as that which intervenes from time to time in the affairs of the Church and the world, as that which is otherworldly and immaterial, and as that which is opposed to materiality, including the materiality of the flesh.

In the light of these dualisms and distortions surrounding Spirit-talk, it may be helpful to say what an experience of the Spirit is *not*. An experience of the Spirit is not the experience of another object alongside other objects, is not an encounter with one more cause alongside other causes, is not an otherworldly item of information alongside worldly information. Too many believers have come to take their experience of the Spirit as some ghostly thing separate from or added to the material and mundane world, something that is distinct from and exterior to the world we see around us. In contrast to this outlook, one author points out:

> The ancient understanding of Spirit (*pneuma*) did not see it as disembodied and lacking materiality. Within the broader Hellenistic world, *pneuma* was conceptualised as an airy substance that had a material quality, but not density.[4]

Conscious of these false impressions about the Spirit, it is instructive to note that another author, the Bishop of Rome, Pope Francis, says in his encyclical on the environment that 'the life of the Spirit is not dissociated from the body or from nature or from worldly realities, but lived in and with them, in communion with all that surrounds us'.[5] Put positively, the Spirit is to be found as embodied in life, present within nature,

---

4. Angela Kim Harkins, 'The Holy Spirit and the New Testament in the light of Second Temple Judaism', in *The Holy Spirit: Setting the World on Fire*, edited by Richard Lennan and Nancy Pineda-Madrid, New York, NY: Paulist Press, 2017, 73–83, at 75.

5. *Laudato Si'*, 216; something similar is said in the same document in a. 98.

and active in worldly realities. In other words, God's Spirit is mediated through the body, through nature, and through the affairs of the world. The natural event portrayed as Moses encountering the burning bush (Exodus 3:21) was not God adding something to the natural world, but a story about how the spirit appears in and through nature for humans. These mediations are 'sacramental' events that reveal and embody the spirit for us in a way a little like the bread and wine of the Eucharist reveal and embody Christ for us. Of course, these embodiments of the Spirit, these mediations of the Spirit, these different expressions of the Spirit, in the Church and in the world are finite, understandable and relative expressions of the Spirit in contrast to the infinite, incomprehensible and absolute mystery of the Spirit in itself.

There is a tendency found in many religions to absolutise finite expressions of the Spirit at the expense of the transcendent mystery that is the Holy Spirit of God. Within every experience of the Spirit, there comes a moment, a mystical moment, in which we must go beyond the finite manifestations of the Spirit into the dazzling darkness of the presence of the infinite Spirit in the world. In the light of these preliminary remarks about what is not an experience of the Spirit, and the suggestion of some principles that might guide the possibility of an experience of the Spirit, we can now move to an examination of what the Bible has to say about the relationship between Spirit and nature. It must be emphasised here that we are only looking at the possibility of 'seeing' the Spirit in nature, and not theologising about the Spirit in the history of Judaism, or in the history of Christianity, or in our understanding of the Trinity.

For many, a theology of the Spirit is associated primarily with the day of Pentecost as recorded in the Acts of the Apostles. Without denying the pivotal importance of this Pentecostal event, it must be noted that the Spirit played a central role in the life of Jesus. To focus only on the day of Pentecost neglects the presence of the Spirit in the life of Jesus and in the life of Israel, as if somehow they were Spirit-less. For too long, and for too many, pneumatology has been seen as the preserve of Christianity to the neglect of the rich theology of the Spirit in Judaism.

However, Jewish scholar John R. Levison points out, correctly in my opinion, that 'Christian Pneumatology becomes less about an exclusive Christian experience or doctrine and more about the presence of God in the great scheme of Israel's history – and Christianity as ancient Israel's heir.'[6] For Levison, 'the essence of Christian Pneumatology, therefore, should be traced back into the heart of the Hebrew scriptures'.[7] When we do this, as we shall see presently, we discover the presence of the Spirit not only in history, but also *in* nature.

The Hebrew word *ruach* is one of the commonly used nouns in the Jewish Bible. It has many shades of meaning which can only be grasped by reference to their context. For some, *ruach* means spirit, wind, or breath.[8] For others, such as Theodore Hiebert, *ruach* has many meanings: atmosphere, breath, the first sacred thing, and the breath of all creatures.[9] This word, *ruach,* is prominent in the Hebrew scriptures. It is found in 378 places, far more than the word 'covenant' (289) or 'mercy' (251). It would be impossible to grasp the uniqueness of Israel without reference to the Hebrew term *ruach.* A succinct statement from Andrew Davis draws together these observations:

> The ancient Israelites understood God as the source of an animating spirit that enlivened all creation.[10]

The Spirit of God gives life not only to human beings, but also to the natural world of plants and animals. The breath of human life derives from, and depends on, God's *ruach,* as does the life of plants and animals and other living species of the natural world. It is one and the same life-giving breath of God that infuses the universe made up of humans, plants and animals, and other living species.

---

6. John R. Levison, *The Jewish Origin of Christian Pneumatology*, The Duquesne University 11th Annual Lecture, 2017, 8.

7. Ibid.

8. See Andrew R. Davis, 'Spirit, Wind, or Breath: Reflections on the Old Testament', in *The Holy Spirit: Setting the World on Fire*, op. cit., 63–72.

9. See Theodore Hiebert, 'Air, the First Sacred Thing: The Conception of *Ruach* in the Hebrew Scriptures', *Exploring Ecological Hermeneutics*, edited by Norman Habel and Peter Trudinger, Atlanta, GA: Society of Biblical Literature, 2008, 9–19.

10. Andrew R. Davis, art. cit., 64.

Before searching the Hebrew scriptures on the Spirit, it may be helpful to look at some primordial experiences of the Spirit in nature as background to a Jewish theology of the Spirit. Here we will confine ourselves to two such experiences. The first experience is the experience of the 'indwelling presence of the Spirit' in nature. There is a presence, a pervasive presence, of the Spirit that dwells in nature. Poets capture this presence of the Spirit in nature better than most theologians. In this regard it is worth quoting nineteenth-century poet Gerard Manley Hopkins (1844–1889). He observes:

> The world is charged with the grandeur of God.
> It will flame out, like shining from shook foil;
> It gathers to a greatness, like the ooze of oil
> Crushed. Why do men then now not wreck his rod?
> Generations have trod, have trod, have trod;
> And all is seared with trade; bleared, smeared with toil; ...
> And for all this nature is never spent;
> There lives the dearest, freshness deep down thing; ...
> Because the Holy Ghost over the bent
> world broods with warm breath and with ah! Bright wings.[11]

This universal presence of the Spirit in nature, in a nature that is 'never spent', is echoed in the Psalms, which also talk about the omnipresence of the Spirit. For example:

> Where can I go from your spirit?
> Or where can I feel from your presence?
> If I ascend to heaven, you are there;
> if I make my bed in Sheol, you are there.
> If I take the wings of the morning
> and settle at the farthest limits of the sea,
> even there your hand shall lead me,
> and your right hand shall hold me fast. (Psalm 139:7–10)

---

11. Gerard Manley Hopkins, 'God's Grandeur', in *The Poetical Works of Gerard Manley Hopkins*, edited by Norman H. MacKenzie, Oxford: Clarendon Press, 1990, 111.

This presence of the Spirit is less something exterior, and far more something interior to the life of nature.

A second primordial experience of the Spirit in nature can be described as the presence of 'a rejuvenating Spirit'. Throughout the life of nature, there is present in nature a spirit that continuously renews the life of the earth through the seasons of the year and the reproductive cycles. What is it that powers and energises and draws this ongoing renewal of nature?

It is the psalmist who senses this ongoing renewal in the following way:

> You cause the grass to grow for the cattle
> and plants for people to cultivate,
> to bring forth food from the earth ... (Psalm 104:14)

And then he goes on to note that:

> When you hide your face, they are dismayed;
> when you take away their breath, they die
> and return to their dust.
> When you send forth your spirit, they are created,
> and you renew the face of the ground. (Psalm 104:29–30)

It is against the background of these primordial experiences of the Spirit and their echo in selected psalms that we can now look more explicitly at the theology of the Spirit in the Hebrew Bible.

b. The Spirit in the Hebrew Bible

Probably the oldest account of the Spirit is found in the Yahwist story of creation in Genesis 2 – a text that goes back somewhere between the tenth and ninth centuries BCE. In verse 7 it is stated:

> ... then the Lord formed man from the dust of the ground,
> and breathed into his nostrils the breath of life; and man
> became a living being. (Genesis 2:7)

Alongside this text, there is the influential sixth-century priestly account of creation in Genesis 1:1–2:

> When God began to create the heavens and the earth, the earth was complete chaos, and darkness covered the face of the deep, while a wind from God swept over the face of the waters. (Genesis 1:1–2)

This text is notoriously difficult to translate. Interpreters are divided on the appropriate translation of the word '*ruach*'. Most English translations (NRSV, NABRE and the New Jewish Publication Society) render '*ruach*' as wind. It is pointed out that the wind here may just be part of the 'formless void' and 'darkness' that preceded the act of creation and, therefore, should not necessarily be thought of as the wind or breath of God. It is further noted that the act of creation is the result primarily of the creative Word (of God) and, therefore, we should not read too much into the use of the word '*ruach*' in this context. On the other hand, there are some, especially among Pentecostal theologians, who argue that the presence of the Spirit of God is the presupposition of the utterance of the Word of God.[12] In support of this particular interpretation, they point to Psalm 33:6, which is explicit about the joint activity of the Spirit and the Word in the act of creation:

> By the *Word of the Lord* the heavens were made
> And all their hosts by the *breath* of his mouth. (italics added)

Clearly, there is room for some debate here, and therefore the opening verses of the priestly account of creation in Genesis 1 can hardly be taken on their own as a foundation for developing a Hebrew theology of the Spirit. There are other texts that should be invoked in any discussion about the role of the Spirit in creation. These include the Psalms, the Book

---

12. See Amos Yong, 'Beginning with the Spirit: Biblical Motifs for a Foundational Pneumatology', in *Spirit – Word – Community: Theological Hermeneutics in Trinitarian Perspective*, Farnham: Ashgate Publishing, 2002, 27–48, at 43–47.

of Job and the Prophet Ezekiel. We will confine ourselves here to some perspectives on the Spirit in Job and Ezekiel. Job says:

> The spirit of God has made me,
> and the breath of the Almighty gives me life. (Job 33:4)

And then, finally:

> If he should take back his spirit to himself
> and gather to himself his breath,
> all flesh would perish together,
> and all mortals return to dust. (Job 34:14–17)

Turning to Ezekiel, the word '*ruach*' is used with a slightly different meaning in the dry bones prophesy of Ezekiel 37:1–14. This text opens:

> The hand of the Lord came upon me and he brought me out by the Spirit (*ruach*) of the Lord and set me down in the middle of the valley.

The text closes:

> I will put my Spirit (*ruach*) within you and you shall live.

The use of '*ruach*' as divine Spirit at the beginning and at the end is consistent. Thereafter, however, it is best translated as 'breath':

> Thus says the Lord God to these bones: I will cause breath
> (*ruach*) to enter you, and you shall live. (5)
> I will lay sinews on you and will cause flesh to come upon
> you and cover you with skin and put breath (*ruach*) in you,
> and you shall live … (6)
> I looked, and there were sinews on them, and flesh had
> come upon them … but there was no breath (*ruach*)
> in them. (8)

Then he said to me, 'Prophesy to the breath (*ruach*), prophesy, mortal, and say to the breath (*ruach*): Thus says the Lord God: Come from the four winds, O breath (*ruach*), and breathe (*ruach*) upon these slain, that they may live. (9) I prophesied as he commanded me, and the breath (*ruach*) came into them ... (10)

The use of *ruach* as breath in these verses shows how flexible the term is and how necessary it is to go beyond a single or a simple translation of *ruach* as Spirit.

Taken together, these selected texts, and many others not mentioned here, add up to a rich, nuanced and differentiated range of meaning attached to the Hebrew word '*ruach*'. That range of meaning includes at least the following points:

- What makes a human alive is their participation in the divine *ruach* (Genesis 2:7; Ezekiel 37:1 and 14; and Isaiah 42:5).
- The *ruach* of God is involved, not only in the lives of humans but also in the lives of other creatures and the life of the earth (Psalm 33:6; Job 34:14–15).
- The gift of life in humans, in other creatures and in the earth comes from the *ruach* of God and depends on the *ruach* of God (Psalm 104:27–30).
- The *ruach* of God comes across as an active energy, empowering the life of nature to be both productive and reproductive (Isaiah 44:3–4).

What is striking about this sketchy summary of this Hebrew theology of the Spirit is that the Spirit is earthly: dwelling in dust, in nostrils, in bodies and in the material elements of air, water, fire and earth. Some commentators talk about the 'earth-loving-spirit',[13] and others refer to 'a

---

13. See Erin Lothes Biviano, 'Elizabeth Johnson and Cantors of the Universe: The Indwelling, Renewing and Moving Creator Spirit and a Pneumatology from Below', in *Turning to*

faith that loves the earth'.[14] It should be emphasised that the mindset of the biblical authors in their treatment of the presence of *ruach* does not allow division, or separation, or split between body and soul, the human and the non-human, nature and spirit. Such dualisms are unbiblical, unfaithful to the text, and foreign to the integrated vision of the Jewish scriptures.[15] It is this underlying unity between Spirit and matter that is an outstanding part of the Hebrew theology of the Spirit and, as such, has a certain resonance with the principle of materiality running through contemporary cosmology, biological evolution and human emergence. As Roger Haight observes, there is 'a material consistency through the galaxies, to our solar system and right down to each single person', and this in turn 'gives the reality of the universe a steady commonality and interrelatedness; everything comes from the same material elements, atoms and sub-atomic principles'.[16]

c. Mark Wallace on the Spirit

These biblical perspectives require a theological translation into an idiom that is not in conflict with contemporary experience, culture and science. One theologian who has taken up this challenge is Mark Wallace, over and above the work of Catholic theologians like Elizabeth Johnson, Denis Edwards and Celia Deane-Drummond. Wallace is acutely aware of the challenges around Spirit-talk, such as the language used and the need to overcome the dogged dualisms between Spirit and matter, body and soul, grace and nature, spirituality and materiality. Part of the challenge is that 'the natural world stands mute until it is spiritually encountered as saturated with grace and meaning'.[17] As we have seen in Chapter 2, the ancient world does not see

the Heavens and the Earth: Theological Reflections on a Cosmological Conversion, Essays in Honour of Elizabeth A. Johnson, edited by Julia Brumbaugh and Natalia Imperatori-Lee, Collegeville, MN: Liturgical Press, 2016, 183.

14. Karl Rahner, *The Mystical in Everyday Life: Sermons, Essays and Prayers*, edited by Annemarie Kidder, New York, NY: Orbis Books, 2010, 52–58.

15. Theodore Hiebert, op. cit., 10 and 17–18.

16. Haight, Roger, 'Spirituality, Evolution, Creator God', in *Theological Studies*, June 2018, 251–73, at 253.

17. Mark Wallace, 'The Song of the Thrush: Christian Animism and the Global Crisis Today', in *The Task of Theology*, New York, NY: Orbis, 2014, 215–34, at 216. I have chosen this particular article by Mark Wallace because it addresses the specific question of this chapter, namely

the earth as dead matter or as some kind of inert substance. Instead, it is infused in varying degrees by the breath of God. Everything that God has made 'in the beginning' is a bearer of the Holy Spirit. In a number of what I call 'preliminary statements' Mark Wallace emphasises that:

- Everything God made is a bearer of the Holy Spirit.[18]
- Nature is a living web of gifted relationships.[19]
- The great expanse of the natural world can be re-envisioned as alive and sacred and thereby deserving of our nurture and love.[20]

On the back of these 'preliminary statements' about the relationship between the Spirit and nature, he opens the way towards a nature-based-pneumatology. He expands these 'preliminary' pneumatological perspectives in the following way:

- God is fully and completely embodied in the natural world.[21]

For Wallace, in his own words:

- The focus falls on the world as thoroughly embodying God's presence.[22]

---

the development of a Spirit-based pneumatology. Wallace has written far more extensively on the Spirit than just this particular article. See especially by Wallace 'The wounded Spirit as the basis for hope in an age of radical ecology', in *Christianity and Ecology: Seeking the well-being of earth and humans*, edited by Dieter T. Hessel and Rosemary Radford Ruether, Harvard, MA: Harvard University Press, 2000, 51–72; and also *Fragments of the Spirit: nature, violence, and the renewal of creation*, New York, NY: Continuum, 1996; and *When God was a Bird: Christianity, animism, and the re-enchantment of the world*, New York, NY: Fordham University Press, 2019. These works would have to be consulted for a fuller treatment of Wallace's theology of the Spirit.

18. Mark Wallace, ibid., 218.
19. Ibid., 219.
20. Ibid.
21. Ibid., 220.
22. Ibid.

He continues:

- Now nothing is held back as God overflows Godself into the bounty of the natural world.[23]

Again, he continues:

- Now all things are bearers of the sacred; each and every creature is a portrait of God, everything that is, is holy.[24]

There is much that is helpful in what I call Wallace's 'preliminary statements' about the Spirit's relationship with nature. Especially useful is his sense that the Spirit is intrinsic to the whole of nature from the beginning of time. This outlook pre-empts some of the dualisms that inhibit the development of pneumatology. Further, these 'preliminary statements' also overcome the expectation of a sporadic intervention by the Spirit in the life of nature. In addition, Wallace has provided a framework that is not in conflict with science.

However, it is the development or expansion of these 'preliminary statements' that will give some readers pause. For example, the application of the words 'fully and completely' to the embodiment of the Spirit in the natural world requires more nuance and qualification. The suggestion that the natural world 'thoroughly' embodies God's presence, that 'nothing is held back' in the overflow of God's self into the world, and that 'every creature is a portrait of God' can raise more questions. If we were to take these 'preliminary statements' at their face value, there would seem to be little or no need for the Incarnation.

There is little doubt that Wallace is seeking to overcome the excesses of Christo-monism by coming up with this radical pneumato-centrism. It is possible that Wallace, in these statements about the Spirit has, unwittingly, overshadowed the uniqueness of the unity of the Word of God in the flesh of Jesus as a child of the cosmos in and through what we call the Incarnation. In addition to these questions concerning Wallace's developed statements about the Spirit in nature, there is a further

---

23. Ibid.
24. Ibid.

ambiguity. There is a consistent tradition in the Bible and the Christian tradition that the Spirit and Word work together jointly. This can be found in the Psalms:

> By the *Word of the Lord* the heavens were made
> and all their host by the *breath* of his mouth. (Psalm 33:6, emphasis added)

This close relationship between the Word and the Spirit is also present in patristic theology. Irenaeus talks about the two hands of God, namely the Word and Spirit, working together. Ambrose talks of the Spirit as 'the author of the Incarnation'. Athanasius (296–377), most explicitly, highlights the unity of the Word and the Spirit. According to Athanasius the Spirit is not outside the Word, but in the Word, and that where the Word is, there the Spirit also is.[25] This focus on the complementarity of the action of the Word and the Spirit is spelt out very clearly in the twentieth century by French theologian Yves Congar. Congar comes up with a guiding principle on the relationship between the Word and the Spirit: 'No Christology without Pneumatology, and no Pneumatology without Christology'.[26] For Congar and others, the action of the Spirit of God must be balanced by the equally important action of the Word of God in creation and redemption. In a discussion about the danger of pneumatocentrism in Joachim of Fiore (1135–1202), Henri de Lubac makes the striking observation: 'Detached from Christ, the Spirit can become almost anything'.[27] Similarly, Kathryn Tanner argues that 'Christ is the key to how the Spirit works'.[28]

---

25. Denis Edwards, 'Sketching an Ecological Theology of the Holy Spirit and the Word of God', in *The Natural World and God: Theological Explorations*, Adelaide: AFT Press, 2017, 43–53, at 45–46. See also D. Edwards, 'Incarnation and the Natural World: Explorations in the Tradition of Athanasius', in *Incarnation: On the Scope and Depth of Christology*, edited by Niels Henrik Gregersen, Minneapolis, MN: Fortress Press, 2015, 157–76.

26. Yves Congar, *The Word and the Spirit*, London: Chapman, 1984, 1.

27. The quotation is taken from Bradford E. Hinze, 'The Spirit in a Trinitarian Ecclesiology', in *Advents of the Spirit: An Introduction to the Current Study of Pneumatology*, edited by Bradford Hinze and D. Lyle Dabney, Marquette, WI: Marquette University Press, 2001, 347–381, at 364.

28. Kathryn Tanner, *Christ the Key*, New York, NY: Cambridge University Press, 2010, 275.

These observations on Mark Wallace's pneumatology highlight the need to outline what the Incarnation of the Word in Jesus adds to his theology of God's Spirit in nature. In answering that question, one would have to propose that the Incarnation of the Word of God in the flesh of Jesus personifies the life of the Spirit that dwells in the natural world. Further, the Incarnation crystalises the universal presence of the Spirit in nature within the drama of the historical life of Jesus. In addition, the death and resurrection of the Word incarnate resonate with the pattern of life, death and rebirth that appears to be built in to the fabric of the world that the Spirit inhabits. An attempt to develop these statements takes us seamlessly into Chapter 6.

CHAPTER 6

A Nature-Based Christology

I see his blood upon the rose
And in the stars the glory of his eyes,
His body gleams amid eternal snows,
I see his face in every flower;
The thunder and the singing of the birds
are but his voice – and carven by his power
rocks are his written words.[1]

OUR POINT of departure for this chapter on Christology is pneumatology. For too long, Christology has been done as if the outpouring
of the Spirit began on the day of Pentecost as described in the Acts of
the Apostles. This outlook bypasses the rich theology of the Spirit in the
Hebrew Bible as sketched in Chapter 5. In support of the move to begin
Christology with pneumatology, one can invoke Congar's principle
enunciated in the last chapter: no Christology without pneumatology
and no pneumatology without Christology. More particularly, appeal can
also be made to the unity that exists in the Bible between the action of
the Spirit and the work of the Word (e.g. Psalm 33:6; Genesis 1:1–3).

---

1. Joseph Mary Plunkett (1887–1916), 'I See His Blood upon the Rose' (1916).

It is also worth noting that Rahner, towards the end of his life, suggested that the gift of the Spirit is the foundation on which Christianity is best understood. He pointed out that 'The divinisation of the world through the Spirit of God is humanly ... the more fundamental conception for Christianity, out of which the Incarnation and Soteriology arise as an inner moment'.[2] In an article on 'Aspects of European Theology' published in German just one year before his death, Rahner proposed the priority of pneumatology over Christology.[3] The context of Rahner's remarks on the primacy of pneumatology is dialogue with other religions. However, the principle enunciated in that article must surely apply also to a theology of creation and the natural world.

Assuming the priority of pneumatology, we can move to the possibility of developing a nature-based Christology. The aim of this chapter is restricted to the development of a theology of the natural world. It will confine itself to the following questions: Does Christology shed any light on the natural world? What does Christology have to offer to our understanding of the natural world? How does Christology enrich our relationship with the natural world? More particularly, what does the preaching of Jesus have to say about the natural world? What is the significance of the historical death and resurrection for our understanding of the rhythms of life within the natural world? Does the Incarnation, especially recent Christologies of Deep Incarnation, have anything to say about the natural world? It is hoped that answers to some of these questions will point us in the direction of constructing a new theology of the natural world, as called for by Mark Harris, John McCarthy, Nancy C. Tuckman and others in Chapters 2 and 3, and, in particular, a new understanding of nature that is profoundly open to nature praising God.

a. From the Quest for the Historical Jesus to the Quest for the Cosmic Christ

In the twentieth century, a lot of time was given to the quest for the historical Jesus. In the twenty-first century that emphasis has shifted to the

---

2. *Karl Rahner in Dialogue, Conversations and Interviews, 1965–1982*, edited by Paul Imhof and Hubert Biallowons, New York, NY: Crossroad, 1986, 126.
3. Karl Rahner, 'Aspects of European Theology', in *Theological Investigations*, vol. XXI, 78–98, at 98.

quest for the cosmic Christ and for a description of the relationship that exists between the Jesus of history and the cosmic Christ of faith. In the context of climate change, the loss of biodiversity and the Covid-19 crisis, we ask: What is the relationship between Jesus and nature? What does Jesus have to say about the natural world? What is the significance of the Incarnation for a theology of nature? Up to now, very little attention was given to the relationship between Jesus and the natural world, beyond the observation that he appealed to nature to talk about the coming reign of God.

It is worth noting that Jesus lived much of his life in close proximity to the natural world:

- He spent forty days in the desert.
- He was with the wild animals in the desert.
- He was baptised in the River Jordan by John the Baptist.
- The transfiguration of Jesus occurred on Mount Tabor.
- He often retired to quiet places of nature to pray.
- He taught on and around the Lake of Galilee.
- He suffered in the Garden of Gethsemane.
- He appeared to Mary Magdalene in the Garden of Resurrection.

These encounters with the natural world had an influence on the life of Jesus. Many of these moments included prayerful communion with God his Father. They left a deep impression on him, so much so that when he taught about the coming reign of God, he drew on his knowledge of the natural world.

In the Synoptics, Jesus shows a remarkable understanding of the natural world. Richard Bauckham lists the following references to animals: birds, camels, chickens, dogs, donkeys, dove, fish, fox, gnat, goat, moth, ox, pig, raven, scorpion, sheep, snake, sparrows, viper, vulture and wolf. Among the plants he refers to: bramble, fig tree, herbs, mulberry, mustard plant, reed, thorns, vine, weeds, wheat and wild flowers. This familiarity with the natural world would have been inspired by, and based on the rich Jewish theology of nature, as found in the Psalms, Genesis, Ezekiel and Job, with which Jesus would have been familiar. Diverse commentators, such as

James Mackey, Roger Haight and Richard Bauckham, talk about the existence of a creation-centred faith in the life of Jesus. The life of Jesus was lived out of a deep Jewish creation-faith and theology. This closeness of Jesus to the natural world and the life of creation does not make him an ecologist before his time, but it does illustrate his awareness of the presence of the Spirit of God in the natural world.[4]

b. The Coming Reign of God and the Renewal of Creation

There can be no doubt about the centrality of the reign of God in the mission and ministry of Jesus. There is, however, a debate about the meaning and range of this key symbol in the life of Jesus. For most commentators, it is about the social influence of the coming reign of God in the lives of people and society, summed up symbolically in the Galilean manifesto in Luke 4:

> 'The Spirit of the Lord is upon me,
> because he has anointed me
> to bring good news to the poor.
> He has sent me to proclaim release to the captives
> and recovery of sight to the blind,
> to set free those who oppressed,
> to proclaim the year of the Lord's favour.' (Luke 4:18–19)

But what, it will be asked, is the relationship between the reign of God and the renewal of creation? Is there any connection, or are these two separate realms? When we take a closer and more critical look at the preaching and praxis of Jesus, we discover that there is a link and a relationship between the coming reign of God and the renewal of creation. It is not as clear as the relationship between the reign of God and renewal of people and society. Nonetheless, the coming reign of God transforms

---

4. Richard Bauckham, 'Reading the Synoptic Gospels Ecologically', in *Ecological Hermeneutics: Biblical, Historical and Theological Perspectives*, edited by David G. Horrell, Cheryl Hunt, Christopher Southgate and Francesca Stavrakopoulou, London: T & T Clark International, 2010, 72–82, at 73 and 78; and Edward Echlin, *Earth Spirituality: Jesus at the Centre*, New Alresford: Arthur James, 1999, 78.

the social order and affects the natural world. This can be seen in a number of different ways.

There are some examples in the Synoptic Gospels which show Jesus speaking out of a rich Jewish theology of creation, informed especially by the Psalms, Genesis 1 and 2, and the Book of Job. As noted, Jesus lived out of a creation-centred faith. For example, he refers to 'Your Father in heaven', who 'makes the sun rise on the evil and on the good, and sends the rain on the righteous and the unrighteous' (Matthew 5:44–45). The coming reign of God is about the coming of the Creator God of the Hebrew Bible, who was deeply involved in the natural world. A similar example can be found in Matthew 10, which talks about two sparrows sold for a penny and 'yet not one of them will fall to the ground apart from your Father ...' (Matthew 10:29–31). God our Father is intimately involved in the life of all creation and not just the lives of human beings.

A more explicit example can be found in Jesus' description of God our Father as 'Lord of heaven and earth' (Matthew 11:25; Luke 10:21). This identification of God our Father as 'Lord of heaven and earth' is also present in the prayer of Jesus: 'Our Father in heaven, hallowed be your name. Your kingdom come, your will be done on earth as it is in heaven' (Matthew 6:9–10). This linking of the coming kingdom of God in the future with the reign of God on earth is significant: it suggests that the coming reign of God embraces the whole of creation as part of the reign of God. Bauckham sums up the meaning of this petition in the Lord's Prayer in the following way: 'The Kingdom of God does not come to extract people from the rest of creation, but to renew the whole of creation in accordance with God's perfect will for it'.[5] The coming reign of God embraces right relationships between human beings and society, but it also includes right relationships between humans and the natural world as part of the renewal of creation. When the Lord of heaven and earth comes to judge the world at the end of time, then the Psalms tell us that creation will rejoice at his advent: 'The heavens will be glad, the earth will rejoice, the sea roar, the fields exult, the trees of the

---

5. Richard Bauckham, ibid., 78.

forest will sing for joy at the coming of the Lord' (Psalm 96:11–13 and Psalm 98:7–9).

On a number of occasions, we find Jesus engaging directly with the natural world. Mark reminds us that Jesus began his public ministry in the wilderness and was with the beasts (Mark 1:13). Another example of Jesus engaging with the natural world can be found in the nature miracles. The story of Jesus walking on the water and stilling the storm resonates with the Genesis story: 'A great windstorm arose, and the waves beat into the boat …' (Mark 4:38). And then, Jesus 'woke up and rebuked the wind and said to the sea, peace and be still. Then the wind ceased, and there was a dead calm' (Mark 4:39). This story echoes with the creation story of Genesis 1:1ff in which God subdues the water of chaos 'in the beginning'. It provokes the question: 'Who then is this that even the wind and sea obey him?' (Mark 4:41).[6] For some, other miracles, such as those of healing, exorcism and nature, point towards a renewal of creation as part of the coming reign of God.

These examples of Jesus engaging with the natural world are slight enough, yet they are sufficient to dispel the view that the reign of God is *only* about the social order. Instead, the coming reign of God, announced by Jesus and realised in part by his actions, embraces not just the social order, but also the natural order. The separation of the social and natural world is something that would have been alien to the Hebrew theology of creation. In Judaism the universe was perceived to be holistic and inclusive, not only of human beings, but also of God's creatures. Creation is a part of the renewal envisaged by Jesus in his preaching and praxis about the coming reign of God, and in his call to conversion that this entails. As Bauckham sums up:

> It is not enough to say the reign of God is about the renewal of all creation, we must say it also includes a renewal of creatures in their inter-relatedness and inter-dependence.[7]

---

6. For a fuller analysis of this particular story, see Richard Bauckham, *Bible and Ecology*, op. cit., 168–71.
7. Ibid., 168.

God has reigned and does reign and will reign not only in the human realm, but also in the natural realm.

c. Overview of the Incarnation

The doctrine of most significance for the development of a theology of nature, however, is the doctrine of Incarnation, especially its development in recent times in terms of what is called Deep Incarnation. It may be helpful to begin our exploration of Deep Incarnation by first of all summarising briefly the traditional meaning of Incarnation. The classical meaning of Incarnation affirms that the eternal Word of God, the second person of the Trinity, became flesh in Jesus of Nazareth. Through his life, death and resurrection Jesus as the Christ saved humanity from itself for new life in community. Here the focus is on the salvation of human beings, with little or no reference to the rest of creation. Within this perspective, there is an emphasis on the unity between God and the humanity of Jesus, described at the Council of Ephesus (431) as a real, hypostatic union. Equally important is the identity of Jesus, as defined by the Council of Chalcedon (451), as truly God (*vere deus*), and truly human (*vere homo*).

The Incarnation of God in Jesus does not mean that Jesus is partly God and partly human. Nor does it mean that Jesus is the result of a confused mixture of divinity and humanity. Instead, God became truly and fully human, while remaining truly and fully God. Further, as Bauckham points out, the Incarnation should not be understood as the entry of God into a world where God was previously absent. Nor is the Incarnation simply a more concentrated form of an already existing divine presence. Instead, the Incarnation 'is a new kind of presence'.[8] Different commentators spell out this new presence of God in the world in Jesus. Some see Jesus as the crystallisation and intensification of a divine presence already given; others see Jesus as the unique, personal form of concentrated creation (E. Schillebeeckx), and still others see Jesus as a microcosm of the macrocosm of the drama of life itself. Here we will restrict ourselves to

---

8. Richard Bauckham, 'The Incarnation and the Cosmic Christ', in *Incarnation: On the Scope and Depth of Christology*, edited by Niels Henrik Gregersen, Minneapolis, MN: Fortress Press, 2015, 25–57, at 36.

two different but complementary ways of articulating this new presence of God in the world.

One expression is a suggestion that the Incarnation of God in Jesus is the visible 'personalisation' of the presence of God already in the world. This presence of God in the world has become personified in the life of Jesus. We can no longer see God as remote, impersonal or distant. The infinite mystery of God has personified God's self in the finite reality of Jesus. The invisible reality of God has been revealed visibly and personally in the flesh of Jesus (1 Timothy 3:16).

Another expression of this new presence of God in the world is found in the particularity of the Incarnation of God in Jesus of Nazareth. There is something striking about the claim that the infinite God of all eternity chose to reveal God's self in the particular person of Jesus, at a particular time in history, in the particular place of Palestine. This is sometimes referred to as 'the scandal of particularity' that is intrinsic to the Christ-event. Something of this 'scandal of particularity' is found in Paul: 'We proclaim Christ crucified, a stumbling block to the Jews and foolishness to the Gentiles, but to those who Christ has called, both Jews and Gentiles, the power of God and the wisdom of God' (1 Corinthians 1:22). What is striking here is that something that is so particular, so specific and so limited could at the same time have universal meaning and far-reaching significance for humanity and creation. There is a dynamic relationship within the Christ-event between the particularity of Jesus the Jew, embodying the personal presence of God, and the universal significance of this 'one-off event' in history for the world. Within the human finitude of Jesus, we encounter the personal presence of the infinite God in the world.

There is a concern among some theologians about appearing to make the particular Incarnation of God in Jesus co-extensive with the universal presence of God in the world. This conflation of the particular presence of God in Jesus with the general presence of God in creation brings the Incarnation close to what theologians call 'pantheism'. In this case, the particular Incarnation of God in Jesus is little more than God's general presence in the world. God and the world become identical, which is the meaning of 'pantheism'.

In contrast to pantheism, theologians put forward what they call 'pan-en-theism', a view which holds that God is present in the world and the world is present in God. There is a mutual indwelling of God in the world and the world in God, but not a mutuality between equal partners. The value of 'pan-en-theism' is that it affirms the absolute transcendence of God alongside the intimate presence of God in the world and in human beings. God is in the world and the world is in God, but there is no conflation or confusion of God with the world, or the world with God. Just as the blood of a mother runs through the veins of her foetus, so that we can fairly say that the child is in the mother and the mother is in the child, so the world is in God and God is in the world, but not reducible, to the natural world.[9] Pan-en-theism brings together the absolute unity of the immanence and transcendence of God in the world and in the Incarnation. What is 'new' about the presence of God in Jesus is the personalisation and particularisation of that divine presence in Jesus.[10]

d. From Incarnation to Deep Incarnation

It is against this background of the traditional meaning of the Incarnation that we can review Niels Henrik Gregersen's theology of Deep Incarnation. Here we can only present, in summarised form, what Gregersen says about Deep Incarnation. Once again, our principle of selectivity is shaped by our interest in working out only a theology of nature and a not a full-fledged Christology. According to a foundational principle in Gregersen, Deep Incarnation means that 'the divine *Logos* ... has assumed not merely humanity, but the whole malleable matrix of materiality'.[11]

---

9. I am indebted to Terrence W. Tilley for this image as a way of overcoming any conflation of God with the world.

10. There is a debate about the difference between the presence of God in the Incarnation and the presence of God in the world. For some, the difference is a difference of kind and, for others, it is a difference of degree. A difference of kind runs the risk of removing God from the human condition and unwittingly denying the humanity of Jesus. A difference of degree runs the risk of reducing the personal and particular presence of Jesus to just another expression of the presence of God in the world. What should not be lost in this debate is what Mark Wallace calls the 'productive contradiction', or the 'coincidence of opposites' or the 'non-oppositional dualism' contained in Chalcedon. See Mark Wallace, 'The Song of the Thrush', art. cit., 225.

11. Niels Henrik Gregersen, 'Deep Incarnation: Why Evolutionary Continuity Matters in Christology', in *Toronto Journal of Theology*, Fall, 2010: 173–87, at 196.

Gregersen spells out the implication of this principle in a number of different articles. He sees Deep Incarnation as the view:

- that 'God's own *Logos* (wisdom and word) was made flesh in Jesus Christ ... by assuming the particular life-story of Jesus the Jew from Nazareth';
- that God 'conjoined the material conditions of creaturely existence (all flesh)';
- that God 'shared and ennobled the fate of all biological life forms (grass and lilies) and experienced the pain of sensitive creatures (sparrows and foxes) from within';
- that 'divine embodiment ... reaches into the roots of material and biological existence as well as the darker side of creation, *Tenebrae creationis*';[12]
- that 'the cross of Christ is here both the apex and depth of Incarnation.[13]

Gregersen sums up his vision of Deep Incarnation in the following succinct statement:

The Incarnation of God in Christ can be understood as a radical or 'deep' Incarnation ... an Incarnation into the very tissue of biological existence and systems of nature.[14]

If we see the Incarnation of the Word of God incarnate in Jesus simply as a one-off, isolated event, separated from the activity of the Word in creation and in the history of Israel, we will miss the full meaning of Deep Incarnation and its far-reaching significance for the natural world. For Gregersen, the flesh assumed by Jesus connects him with all human

---

12. Niels Henrik Gregersen, 'The Extended Body of Christ: Three Dimensions of Deep Incarnation', in *Incarnation: On the Scope and Depth of Christology*, edited by Niels Henrik Gregersen, Minneapolis, MN: Fortress Press, 2015: 225–51, at 225–26.

13. Niels Henrik Gregersen, 'The Cross of Christ in an Evolutionary World', in *Dialog: A Journal of Theology*, 40, 2, 2001, 192–207; and Niels Henrik Gregersen, 'Christology', in *Systematic Theology and Climate Change: Ecumenical Perspectives*, edited by Michael Northcoff and Peter M. Scott, London: Routledge, 2014, 33–50.

14. Ibid.

beings, with the entire community of the earth (that is all flesh), and with the materiality of the cosmos in all its dynamic processes.[15] Denis Edwards sums up the sweep of Gregersen's Deep Incarnation:

> The flesh of Jesus is made from the atoms born in the processes of nucleo-synthesis in the stars, and shaped by 3.7 billion years of evolution on earth.[16]

Gregersen talks about the Incarnation in at least three other different senses: in a strict sense, where Incarnation applies to Jesus Christ, in his lifetime, and in the Church as the body of Christ; in a second sense, a broad sense, the Incarnation of God in Jesus is about Jesus sharing the depth and scope of the social and geo-biological conditions of the entire cosmos;[17] in a third sense, what he calls the soteriological sense of Incarnation, which unites the strict and broad sense of Incarnation in which Christ 'co-suffers with and for all suffering creatures'.[18]

Located within this wider context, Deep Incarnation has radical *implications* for the way we see, relate to and value nature. In this perspective, nature is in receipt of the saving embrace of the Word of God made flesh in Jesus, and this changes our underlying relationship with the natural world. Further, Deep Incarnation builds a bridge between Christology, evolutionary biology and ecology.

Another approach to the Incarnation can be found in the work of Irish biblical scholar Margaret Daly-Denton, author of *John: An Earth Bible Commentary*. In her analysis, she is clear that, 'For the biblically literate Jewish audiences, Word and Wisdom would have been two ways of talking about the same reality, two terms used metaphorically to convey God's activity in creation and sustaining of the world'.[19] Our focus here

15. See Denis Edwards, *Deep Incarnation: God's Redemptive Suffering with Creatures*, New York, NY: Orbis Books, 2019, 113.

16. Ibid.

17. Niels Henrik Gregersen, '*Cur Deus Caro*: Jesus on the Cosmic Story', in *Theology and Science*, 11, no. 4, 2013, 370–93, at 385.

18. Ibid., 386.

19. Margaret Daly-Denton, *John: An Earth Bible Commentary: Supposing Him to be the Gardener*, London: Bloomsbury T&T Clark, 2017, 32.

is on the Word made flesh who lived among us and its implications for a theology of the natural world as subject.

According to Daly-Denton the Word made flesh connects the Word 'with all of flesh's ... interconnectedness within the whole biotic community of life on earth'.[20] Further, 'the biblical understanding of *sarx* may well urge us ... to read the "us" among whom the Word pitched his tent as the whole earth community and not just human beings'.[21] In other words, flesh in the Bible is broader than humanity, and, lest we forget, living matter is connected to the whole material environment from which it evolved. In becoming flesh, the Word is incarnate in the whole natural world.

These commentaries by Gregersen and Daly-Denton are mutually enhancing for the development of a theology of the natural world. The outreach of the Word made flesh embraces the person of Jesus, the whole of humanity, and the whole biotic community of life on earth. For Daly-Denton, Incarnation reminds us 'that everything in creation was intended by God to be a revelation, a communication, a "*logos*" so to speak, a Word from God for human beings to hear, heed and reflect upon'.[22]

In the light of this sketch of Deep Incarnation and an earth-conscious reading of the Prologue of John's Gospel, we can begin to see the significance of Incarnation for a new theology of the natural world, a new appreciation of the divine depth of nature, and the recovery of a number of *qualities* as intrinsic to the life of nature. The application of these qualities to the life of nature transforms the way we experience and relate to the world around us. What are these particular qualities and how do we name them? At best we can outline only some of them here.

Deep Incarnation retrieves the value, *the intrinsic value*, of the natural world in itself and in the sight of the Creator;[23] provides a basis for the recovery of the integrity, what Bauckham calls '*the independent integrity*' of the natural world; recovers the *sacred character of the natural world* as

---

20. Ibid., 35.
21. Ibid.
22. Ibid., 34.
23. See Richard Bauckham, 'Incarnation and the Cosmic Christ', op. cit., 46–47.

implied in the Jewish theology of creation; paves the way for the development of *an incarnational theology* of the natural world.

Moreover, according to Celia Deane-Drummond, Deep Incarnation is a call 'to act out in *proper respect for the natural world and all its creatures*';[24] a challenge to 'humanity *to reconsider its place in the natural world*'; a recognition of 'the close dependence of human beings on the natural world'; and a recovery 'of how *peace between people pre-supposes peace with the natural order*'.[25]

In addition, Deep Incarnation stands out as a *critique of the death of nature* lamented by Caroline Merchant, in the mechanisation of nature by modernity, and the subsequent disenchantment of the universe; it 'confers dignity ... on everything and everyone, past and present'[26]; it *sanctifies the biophysical world*, making all things meaningful and valuable in the divine scheme';[27] it provides a new valuation on the underlying unity of the flesh of Jesus with the flesh of the whole of humanity and the flesh of the biotic community of life on earth;[28] and it offers a wider context for recovering *the meaning of the cosmic Christ*, emphasised in Pauline literature, especially in Colossians and Ephesians, as well as the Johannine *Logos* Christology, which we will look at presently.

To put all of this in a slightly different way, we can say that Deep Incarnation overcomes any separation between the theology of creation and Christology while preserving their distinct perspectives. It introduces a new consonance between science and Christology, and opens up the possibility of a new dialogue between Christology and science. It also makes it possible for nature to become a proper object of theological reflection. In this way, we can move from an overly anthropocentric theology towards the development of a Christo-centric universe, a universe centred on God who, through the Incarnation,

24. Celia Deane-Drummond, 'The Wisdom of Fools: A Theo-Dramatic Interpretation of Deep Incarnation', in *Incarnation: On the Scope and Depth of Christology*, 177–201, at 199 (italics added).

25. Ibid.

26. James A. Nash, *Loving Nature: Ecological Integrity and Christian Responsibility*, Nashville, TN: Abingdon Press, 1991, 109.

27. Ibid.

28. Margaret Daly-Denton, op. cit., 34–35.

participates in the inter-connectedness of the whole living community of creation.

No treatment of the Incarnation would be adequate without some further analysis, however brief, of the Prologue of John's Gospel as complementary to Gregersen and Daly-Denton's theology of Deep Incarnation. We will confine ourselves here to an overview of the influential Johannine Christology of John's Gospel. Again, our comments on the *Logos* Christology of John will be constrained by our interest in working towards a theology of the natural world. The *Logos* Christology of John's Gospel is interpreted by most as a cosmic hymn of praise, in terms of the eternal Word of God entering into personal engagement with the whole of creation and the history of all creatures symbolised by the word 'flesh'. Some of the key verses in this fourteen-verse hymn are as follows:

> In the beginning was the Word, and the Word was with God, and the Word was God. (1)
> He was in the beginning with God. (2)
> All things came into being through him, and without him not one thing came into being. (3)
> What has come into being in him was life, and the life was the light of all people. (4)
> The light shines in the darkness, and the darkness did not overtake it. (5)
> And the Word became flesh and lived among, and we have seen his glory ... (14)

Many background influences are at play in the composition of this unique Christological hymn: the Jewish theology of the Word, the centrality of Wisdom within Judaism, the Hellenistic philosophy of *logos* and its many variants. The hymn starts out 'in the beginning', clearly echoing 'in the beginning' in the opening verses of Genesis 1:1, and again in the second verse we are told 'he was in the beginning with God', which is an explicit reference to Wisdom who was present to God 'at the first, before the beginning' (Proverbs 22:22–31, at 22–23). This echo of Genesis continues in the Prologue through the images of life, light and darkness (Genesis 1:4–5). This cosmic activity of the Word comes to a climax with the eternal Word descending into human history in verse 14: 'And the Word was made flesh and lived among us and we have seen His glory'.

These verses of John's Prologue have been analysed through the centuries, and will continue to be exegeted until the Eschaton because of the multi-layered, complex history attached to the words *Logos* (Word) and *sarx* (flesh). It should be noted that the *Logos*/Word did not become a human being (*homo*), nor did the Word become a man (*vir*); instead, and far more radically, verse 14 claims that 'the *Logos* became *sarx*'. Everything hinges around the multiple meanings attached to the word '*sarx*'. This word 'flesh'/'*sarx*' 'is wider and deeper than 'human being'. From a biblical point of view, the flesh/*sarx* means at least the whole of the human being, and not just the soul or the spirit, but also the whole corporeal reality of what is involved in being human: materiality, weakness, perishability, transience, vulnerability and mortality. The expression 'all flesh' appears in the Bible to remind us that the human belongs to all other creatures and the wider flesh-community of creation. There is a growing consensus that flesh means not only the full reality of a human being, but also the whole material and biological reality of creation, as brought out by Gregersen and Daly-Denton. The eternal Word of God has entered into the whole of creation in its beauty and brutality as well as the particular intensity of the life and death of every human being, and the life, death and rebirth of the natural world as a rhythm that appears to be built in to the very structure of reality itself.

In this way, the outreach of the *Logos* in John's Gospel includes the whole of the natural world. According to Gregersen and Daly-Denton, the entry of the *Logos* in and through the Incarnation embraces the history of the materiality of nature and the biological life of humanity. In this sense the doctrine of the Incarnation is of profound significance for the construction of a theology of the natural world. In effect, the natural world, alongside humanity, is the object of God's embrace in the Incarnation.

It now begins to appear that Deep Incarnation provides a new lens through which it becomes possible to retrieve the significance of the creation-centred Christologies of Paul and John for the twenty-first century. Deep Incarnation also opens the way to talk about the presence of the cosmic Christ throughout the natural world.

e. From Deep Incarnation to a New Theology of Nature as Subject and Agent

If we weave together these *implications* of Deep Incarnation for nature, then we are taking an important step in the construction of a new theology of the natural world. The recognition of the intrinsic value of nature, the independent integrity of nature, the proper respect due to nature, and an appreciation of nature as an appropriate object of theological reflection gives us the beginnings of a new narrative about nature.

The recognition of these different *qualities* of nature, however, begs the following kind of questions: Where do these qualities of nature reside? What is the source of these qualities? Where do these qualities of nature originate? There are different ways of answering these questions.

The ultimate answer is that these qualities of nature derive from the Creator God who declared seven times that all that God had made 'was good' (Genesis 1:3, 10, 12, 18, 21, 25). The dignity of nature derives not only from a theology of creation but also from the eschatological orientation of nature to become part of the new creation in Christ (2 Corinthians 5:17 and Galatians 6:15) and part of the promised new heaven and the new earth to come (Leviticus 21:1–3; 2 Peter 3:13). This intrinsic dignity of nature derives from its origins and its eschatological destiny in Christ.

One immediate answer to these questions requires that we review the way we look at reality. The short-sighted, empirical project of modernity sees reality as static, inert and lifeless matter, to be exploited by humans for humans. There is another, alternative, way of looking at reality. Teilhard de Chardin captures this alternative way in the following quotation:

> It is a fact, beyond question, that deep within ourselves we can discern, as though through a rent, an 'interior' at the heart of things; and this glimpse is sufficient to force upon us the

conviction that in one degree or another this 'interior' exists and has always existed in nature.[29]

For Teilhard, interiority exists not only in human beings, but also in nature. In brief, he argues that 'the time has come for us to realise that any interpretation of the universe must cover the inside as well as the outside – spirit as well as matter'.[30]

A similar point of view can be found in Thomas Berry, who was influenced to some degree by Teilhard, though they did differ on other issues. In a well-known quotation, already used in Chapter 3, Berry points out that 'The universe is not a collection of objects, but a community of subjects.'[31] For Berry, there are varying degrees of subjectivity within the universe, including subjectivity within nature.

These themes of interiority and subjectivity are taken up more extensively by John F. Haught. In his landmark book *The New Cosmic Story: Inside Our Awakening Universe*, Haught suggests that some form of subjectivity was present in the beginning of evolution, and that this subjectivity unfolded in the 'flowering of subjectivity'[32] that erupted into the light of human consciousness with the advent of the human. With the appearance of the human, subjectivity reached an unprecedented pitch of intensity. Echoing Teilhard, Haught argues that the inside story of interiority/subjectivity/consciousness needs to be told if we are to understand the outside of the world in which we are all enmeshed. Haught sees 'interiority as part of nature',[33] and so he talks about the sky, the sun, stars, rivers, the rain, mountains and rocks as 'pulsed with an inner life'.[34]

Alongside this existence of some degree of interiority, subjectivity and consciousness within the natural world, there is also a growing

29. Pierre Teilhard de Chardin, *The Human Phenomenon*, translated by Sarah Appleton-Webber, Eastbourne: Sussex Academic Press, 1999, 57–58.

30. Ibid., 6.

31. Thomas Berry, *The Great Work: Our Way into the Future*, New York, NY: Random House, 1999, 82.

32. John F. Haught, *The New Cosmic Story: Inside our Awakening Universe*, New Haven, CT: Yale University Press, 2017, 71.

33. Ibid., 70.

34. Ibid., 131.

recognition of the need to posit the existence of some form of agency within nature. It is empirically evident that we live in a world of constant action and reaction, of cooperation and competition, of integration and disintegration. These interactions are plain to see in terms of the ongoing construction and deconstruction that takes place in the human world.

Commentators on the environmental crisis suggest that climate change, the loss of biodiversity, and now the global health pandemic point towards the existence of some form of agency. As the US-based Indian writer Amitav Ghosh observes:

> As we watch the environmental and biological disasters unfolding across the earth, it is becoming harder to hold on to the belief that the planet is an inert body that exists merely to provide humans with resources.[35]

For Ghosh, humanity is faced with 'the task of imaginatively restoring agency and voice to non-human'.[36] The word 'restore' is well chosen here. In biblical times the natural world, as we have seen in Chapter 1, had agency and voice, but this became muted with the rise of modernity, which gave us a dis-enchanted universe.

Bruno Latour, a French philosopher-sociologist, is clear that what is now needed is a new story of the earth that takes account of the existence of an 'agitated and sensitive earth'.[37] Some philosophers of science are also proposing the presence of agency within the natural world. Canadian philosopher Denis Walsh sees agency as a broad-based category in the natural world that has enormous consequences in the biosphere and the anthroposphere. The problem, clearly articulated by Walsh, is that modern science has been blind to agency, seeing the natural world as a machine moved by causes and effects.[38]

---

35. Amitav Ghosh, *The Nutmeg's Curse: Parables for a Planet in Crisis*, Chicago, IL: University of Chicago Press, 2021, 83.
36. Ibid., 204.
37. Bruno Latour, 'Agency at the Time of the Anthropocene', in *New Literary History*, 45, 2018, 1–18, at 3.
38. Denis Walsh, 2018–2019 Paris IAS fellow, online video, 2021.

Commenting on the need for a new story about the earth and the need to recognise some form of agency within the natural world, Michael S. Northcroft sums up aspects of this debate in the following way:

> The missing element in contemporary human ethics and politics is the recognition of agency of other creatures … in generating and sustaining the conditions of life on earth that make it uniquely habitable for humans.[39]

The US Franciscan theologian Dan Horan is also concerned to retrieve the category of agency within a theology of the natural world. He suggests persuasively that the presence of 'an anthropocentric privilege' within the modern mindset has removed the possibility of subjectivity and agency from the natural world.[40] In particular the interpretation of the human made in the image and likeness of God (*Imago Dei*) has had a negative impact on our relationship with the natural world. As a corrective Horan seeks to recover the existence within the natural world of what he calls 'non-human creaturely agency.'[41] He does this by expanding the doctrine of the *Imago Dei* to embrace the whole of creation rather than something exclusive to human beings. He achieves this by invoking the analogical imagination to understand the existence of different degrees of agency within the natural world. He notes how certain features – cognition, moral reasoning and emotion – once thought to be exclusive to humanity can be found in varying degrees in the non-human world. In effect, we can no longer see agency as exclusive to human beings, but rather as something present in different ways in the natural world. To support this recognition of the importance of agency, Horan calls for a rereading of the Book of Genesis.[42]

---

39. Michael S. Northcroft, 'Ecology and Hope', pdf, 19 pages, Universitas Gadjah Mada, Indonesia, available at https: www.academia.edu.
40. Daniel P. Horan, 'Deconstructing Anthropocentric Privilege: *Imago Dei* and Non-human Agency', in *Heythrop Journal*, 60, 2019: 560–70.
41. Horan, art. cit., 560.
42. Daniel P Horan, 'Creation', in *T&T Clark Handbook of Theological Anthropology*, edited by Mary Ann Hinsdale IHM and Stephen Okey, New York, NY: T&T Clark, 2021, 49–59.

For example he shows how a rereading of Genesis 1:1–28 reveals a closer relationship between humanity and non-human creation than we thought up to now. He points out that there are neglected 'parallels and continuities between human beings and non-human creation'.[43] He notes how God commanded human beings 'to be fruitful and multiply and fill the earth'.[44] In a similar way, God blessed non-human creation and said to them: 'be fruitful and multiply, and fill the waters in the seas, and let the birds multiply on the earth'.[45] Horan interprets these parallels and continuities between humans and non-humans as pointing towards 'the divine bestowal of creative agency to all living things'.[46] He goes further by suggesting that we can talk about some form of co-creativity between God and all living beings. Until recently such co-creativity was seen as something reserved for the relationship between God and human beings. This refocusing on the co-creativity between God and the whole of creation is facilitated by the retrieval of agency. It should be noted in passing that a close relationship exists between agency and co-creativity.

Further, this co-creativity between God and the whole of creation, and not just with human beings, seems also to be present in the account of God's universal covenant with creation in Genesis 9. There is a refrain in this biblical account of God's universal covenant with creation in Genesis 9: 8–17. There we find God saying: 'I will establish my covenant with every living creature' (10, 12, 15, and 16) and with 'all flesh' (11, 15, 16, and 17). This affirmation of a universal covenant between God and every living creature also points, like Genesis 1:1–28, towards the existence of some form of agency within non-human creation.

This rediscovery of non-human human agency is another important step on the way to coming to grips with the possibility of nature praising God. The point of this discussion is to highlight not only the possibility of agency but its necessity if we are to understand a little better what is going on in the world around us, especially in relation to the climate crisis but also regarding the possibility of nature praising God. The positing of

---

43. Ibid., 55.
44. Genesis 1:1–28.
45. Genesis 1:1–22.
46. Horan 'Creation', art. cit., 53.

agency within the natural world is complementary to the recognition of interiority, subjectivity and consciousness within human beings.

This introduction to some philosophical and theological emphases on agency, merely sketched here, confirms the legitimacy of the founding question of this book: How is it possible for nature to praise God? Without a recognition of some form of agency within the natural world, the possibility of nature praising God is all the more difficult to understand, whereas with the recognition of agency in the natural world we have one more building block in making sense of nature praising God.

CHAPTER 7

Integrating a Theology of Creation in the Service of Liturgy

We have only begun to love the earth
we have only begun to imagine the fullness of life
How can we tire of hope?
– So much is in bud
How can desire fail?
– We have only begun to imagine justice and mercy
Surely our river cannot already be hastening into
the sea of nonbeing?

Not yet, not yet – there is too much broken that must be mended
too much hurt we have done to each other
We have only begun to know the power that is in us
if we could join
Our solitudes in the communion of struggle.

So much is unfolding that must complete its gesture,
So much is in bud.[1]

---

1. Denise Levertov, 'Beginners', in *Candles in Babylon,* Cambridge, MA: New Directions Publishing Corporation, 1982.

WE HAVE been emphasising the importance of a theology of creation as the context for understanding nature praising God and the development of a theology of the natural world. We must now explore a more integrated theology of creation that is not only amenable to understanding nature praising God, but also contains lessons for a more holistic renewal of liturgy in the twenty-first century.

A Christian theology of creation will be grounded in the Christ-event, either as a point of departure or as a point of arrival. The person of Christ, crucified and risen, will be at the centre of a Christian theology of creation. For too long, in the twentieth century, creation and Christology were separate tracts in theology. Christ often appeared as an appendix to creation, and this in turn often gave rise to deistic tendencies and a disenchanted view of the universe. There are a number of creation-centred Christologies in the New Testament, such as the new creation in Christ (2 Corinthians 5:17 and Galatians 6:15); the groaning of creation (Romans 8:18–25), and the exaltation Christologies (Philippians 2:5–11). We will restrict ourselves here to Colossians 1:15.

There are three moments within this Christological hymn that are central: first of all Christ, the image of the invisible God, is identified as 'the first-born of all creation' and not simply of humanity, but of *all* creation. The first-born in the biblical traditions connotes a primacy of function within a kinship structure and not just a primacy of place.[2] In other words, the 'focus here is not on his relationship with the rest of the human race, but with the entire cosmos'.[3]

The second moment is when the author of Colossians states: 'For in him all things, in heaven and on earth … were created' (v. 15). Here, the emphasis is, as in the first moment, on the all-inclusive character of the Christ-event. Lest there be any misunderstanding, the author of Colossians spells out the meaning of 'all things': 'Things in heaven and on earth; things visible and invisible' (Colossians 1:16). There is an awareness of the interconnectedness of all things, including the intrinsic relationship between nature and human beings.[4]

2. See Dianne Bergant, *A New Heaven, A New Earth: The Bible and Catholicity*, New York, NY: Orbis Books, 2016, 154.

3. Ibid.

4. Ibid., 156.

The third moment in Colossians comes in the statement that: 'All things have been created through him and for him' (Colossians 1:16). Once again, the vision is one of inclusivity, highlighting the unity of Christ with the whole of nature and humanity. Christ is the agent through whom God creates, and Christ is the goal of all creation.

Within this hymn, there is no separation of humanity from nature, no isolation of the natural world from the human world. For this reason, this Christological hymn, probably sung within the liturgical assembly of the Colossians, is usually described as the cosmic hymn of Colossians. A fuller account of a Christ-centred theology of creation would have to deal with similar perspectives within John 1:1–14; 1 Corinthians 8:6; Ephesians 1:3–10; Philippians 2:5–11.

The classical theology of creation is grounded, as already seen, in the joint activities of the Creator Spirit and the Word in bringing about the creation of the universe. Against this background, and out of this context, there also emerged a multi-layered theology of creation summed up in terms of original creation, the ongoing gift of creation and the promise of a new creation. These three dimensions of creation are sometimes, unhelpfully in my view, abbreviated into a theology of 'creation out of nothing'. Strictly speaking, these three dimensions of creation are mutually complementary and interdependent, though they often become disconnected. We will begin with an exploration of the doctrine of creation out of nothing and then move to the meaning of the gift of ongoing creation and the promise of a new creation.

a. Retrieving the Theology 'Creation out of Nothing'

The doctrine of creation out of nothing (*creatio ex nihilo*) is a core teaching in Judaism, Christianity and Islam. It claims that God created the world out of nothing and not, therefore, as some tried to say in the past, from some form of pre-existent matter, space or time. This doctrine stands out deliberately against certain misinterpretations of Genesis 1, which suggest that God created the world from 'a formless void' and 'darkness over the face of the deep'. Creation out of nothing explicitly differs from the prevailing views at that time about the origins of the world, namely that God created the world out of pre-existing matter, space or time because, as was held at that time, 'out of nothing comes nothing'. Creation out of nothing is an intrinsic part of Christian faith, yet it has not been prominent in our understanding of Christian faith and identity. Many would hold that creation out of nothing is central, not only to the theology of creation, but also to Christology, eschatology and liturgy. We will confine ourselves to its importance for a theology of the natural world.

Creation out of nothing is not a rival, or an alternative, to the scientific theories of different cosmologies. *Creatio ex nihilo* is less a theory of origins and more a theology about the relationship that exists between God and the universe in the past, present and future. This doctrine is not therefore about cosmology but about theology. Creation out of nothing seeks to safeguard the radical difference between God and creation on the one hand, while acknowledging at the same time, the existence of a relationship of absolute dependency of creation on God. This doctrine, therefore, is as much about the present and the future as it is about the past. It is intimately bound up with the monotheism of Judaism, Christianity and Islam. In making these statements about God creating out of nothing, we must also acknowledge the limits surrounding what we are saying. Strictly speaking, God cannot be described or conceptualised or objectified in the ways in which we describe finite beings: God is not a being alongside other beings, and is not a cause alongside other causes. When we talk about God creating out of nothing, we are talking about the action of God symbolically, dialectically and analogically. These introductory comments beg the obvious questions: Why is the doctrine of creation so important? What does creation out of nothing tell us about God?

This doctrine affirms the transcendence and immanence of God. It also holds that there is no coercion or compulsion or necessity in the divine act of creation in the past, in the present or in the future. This doctrine asserts the sovereign freedom of God in creating and continuing to create and hold the world together. The act of creation is an utterly gratuitous act of love by God. It is an expression of the creativity, graciousness and freedom of God on the one hand and, on the other hand, the absolute dependence of everything on God.[5] This doctrine of creation

---

5. Janet Soskice, '*Creatio ex Nihilo*: Its Jewish and Christian Foundations', in *Creation and the God of Abraham*, edited by David B. Burrell and others, Cambridge: Cambridge University Press, 2010, 24–39, at 38.

out of nothing affirms that creation is a gift, that individual existence is pure gift, and continues to be gift as much in the present as in the past. Without a sense of creation as gift and grace, there would be no worship. As Simon Oliver notes, a gift, to be truly a gift, must be unwrapped and explored. The theology of *creatio ex nihilo* is one way, an important way, of opening up and exploring the unity of the original gift of creation, the ongoing gift of existence, and the promise of what is to come. Without that exploration, the gift of creation and the grace of human existence run the risk of being a mere commodity, admired today and forgotten tomorrow.[6]

It should also be emphasised that creation out of nothing offers key reasons for the praise and worship of God within Judaism, Christianity and Islam. Janet Soskice, on more than one occasion, has highlighted this link between creation out of nothing and the act of worship. She notes that: '*creatio ex nihilo* has been dear to all who worship the God of Abraham'.[7] Elsewhere, she points out that creation out of nothing is: 'a response by Jews and Christians to a fundamental question: who is the God we worship?'[8] Or 'who is this God to whom we pray?'[9] This doctrine, creation out of nothing, 'undergirds so much of what Christians have wanted to say about prayer, providence, beauty, divine presence, freedom and grace'.[10] It is important to note that the doctrine of creation out of nothing is not per se a philosophical point of view, but the outcome of the historical revelation of God in the Jewish and Christian scriptures. As Soskice points out, the doctrine is not 'in the Bible' but is biblically inspired by the Psalms (e.g. Psalms 124 and 33:9) and other texts like Judith 16:14 and 1 and 2 Maccabees, and, in the New Testament, 1 Corinthians 8:6, Colossians 1:15–16 and John 1:1–14.[11] In brief,

---

6. Simon Oliver, 'Every Good and Perfect Gift is from Above: Creation *ex nihilo* before Nature and Culture', in *Knowing Creation: Perspectives from Theology, Philosophy and Science,* Vol.1, Andrew B. Torrance and Thomas H. McCall (eds.), Grand Rapids, MI: Zondervan, 2018, 27–45, at 39–40.

7. Janet Soskice, '*Creatio ex Nihilo*: Its Jewish and Christian Foundations', op. cit., 25.

8. Janet Soskice, 'Why *Creatio ex Nihilo* for Theology Today?', op. cit., 37–54, at 40.

9. Ibid., 41.

10. See Janet Soskice, 'Introduction', in *Modern Theology* (Special issue: 'Creation '*Ex Nihilo*' and Modern Theology'), April 2013, 1.

11. Janet Soskice, 'Why *Creatio ex Nihilo* for Theology Today', art. cit., 48–57.

according to Soskice, creation out of nothing is 'a biblically compelled piece of metaphysical theology'.[12]

b. Continuous Creation

So far, we have focused largely on creation out of nothing. This foundational theology of creation must be followed up by another aspect to creation, namely that original creation continues in the present and this is often referred to as 'continuous creation'. Creation out of nothing is not a once-off event, but rather a continuous act that holds the universe together. If, for one moment, God withdrew his act of creation out of nothing, then the world would return to nothing. It is continuous creation that drives home that every single moment of existence is an ongoing gift. We must, therefore, move beyond a deistic theology of creation. The God of creation is not an absentee landlord who built his home and then departed the stage. Instead, God is continuously involved, and intimately co-present in ongoing creation as gift. This ongoing, creative co-presence of God to creation is captured by Herbert McCabe in the following metaphor. The Creator 'makes all things and keeps them in existence from moment to moment, not like a sculptor who makes a statue and leaves it alone, but like a singer, who keeps her song in existence at all times'.[13] It is in the doctrine of continuous creation that the importance of the link between pneumatology and creation comes into focus.

c. The Promise of a New Creation

This continuous co-presence of God to ongoing creation carries within its ambit the promise of a new creation in the light of the Christ event. This new creation is not about the annihilation of the old creation; it is instead a transformation of the old into something new. This is symbolised in the New Testament in terms of the new creation in Christ (2 Corinthians 5:17 and Galatians 6:15) and the promise of a new heaven and a

---

12. Janet M. Soskice, *'Creatio ex Nihilo*: Its Jewish and Christian Foundations', in *Creation and the God of Abraham*, ed. by David Burrell, Carlo Cogliati, Janet M. Soskice and William R. Stoeger, Cambridge: Cambridge University Press, 2010, 24–39, at 25.
13. Herbert McCabe, *God, Christ and Us*, edited by Brian Davies, New York, NY: Continuum, 2003, 103. Quotation taken from Elizabeth A. Johnson, 'Is God's Charity Broad Enough?', in *Irish Theological Quarterly*, 2015, No. 4, 286.

new earth (Revelation 21:1–5, and 2 Peter 3:13). This means, most importantly, that creation has a destiny, and that this destiny has been revealed in the Christ-event: in the preaching and teaching of Jesus concerning the coming reign of God, and the insight that the reign of God has been realised *in embryo* in the historical death and bodily resurrection of Jesus from the dead. In other words, the foundational unity of the life, death and bodily resurrection of Jesus holds out the promise of a new Creation in Christ.

Rahner spells this out in the following way: 'Resurrection is the beginning of the transformation of the world' and 'in this beginning the destiny of the world is already in principle decided and has already begun'.[14] This condensed statement will only make sense in the twenty-first century in the light of a number of background assumptions. The first of these is the acceptance of the biblical view of creation as a holistic, integrated and unified vision of the universe, especially as outlined in Genesis 1 and 2, the Psalms, the Book of Job, Ezekiel and Deutero-Isaiah. What happens in one part of the universe affects, directly or indirectly, the rest of the universe. A second assumption is the acceptance of a profound unity between Spirit and matter. This is brought out most persuasively in Teilhard de Chardin's fascination with matter. In 1919, he wrote an article on 'The Spiritual Power of Matter', which concluded with a twenty-verse 'Hymn to Matter'.[15] He returned to this vision in 1936 when he wrote:

All that exists is matter becoming
There is neither spirit nor matter in the world;
(Instead) the stuff of the universe is Spirit-matter
No other substance but this could produce the human
    molecule.[16]

---

14. Karl Rahner, 'Resurrection: D. Theology', in *Sacramentum Mundi: An Encyclopedia of Theology*, New York, NY: Herder & Herder, 1970, 332–33, at 333.

15. Pierre Teilhard de Chardin, 'The Spiritual Power of Matter', in *Hymn of the Universe*, London: Collins, 1965, 68–71.

16. Teilhard de Chardin, *Human Energy*, London: Collins, 1969, 57–58.

De Chardin's view of the unity of Spirit and matter is inspired by a biblically based pneumatological understanding of creation, and at the same time is informed by his scientific understanding of the universe. Another assumption in Rahner is the presence of new directions opened up by contemporary cosmologies. Without buying into the details of modern cosmologies, we can accept the broad direction and consensus opened up by the new cosmic stories. There is a movement from the Big Bang cosmologies 13.8 billion years ago, to the emergence of biological life some 5 billion years ago, and the unique appearance of self-conscious human beings roughly 200,000 years ago.

If cosmologists can move from matter to biological life to the existence of human life, is it all that incredible to move from the gift of human existence to the promise of a new creation in Christ in the light of the Paschal Mystery of the unity of the life, death and bodily resurrection of Jesus from the dead? Some scientists talk about the evolutionary trajectory from cosmic dust to human existence, others see the human as cosmic dust in a state of consciousness. If we can move from cosmic dust to embodied consciousness, can we not move from reflective self-consciousness to bodily resurrection?

We can imagine cosmic dust evolving. We can imagine sentient non-humans as our ancestors, but they could not imagine the sorts of mind we would develop. We may not be able to imagine with any accuracy what bodily resurrection will be, but we can imagine such a future growing out of the present. After all, in the past, unimaginable futures have emerged; why assume that that trajectory is exhausted? In suggesting these transformative jumps within history, within evolutionary history, it must be stated once again, especially in reference to the bodily resurrection, that we are talking metaphorically/symbolically/analogically.

The promise of the new creation in Christ is beyond human comprehension. At best, we can only employ worldly images to suggest that which is both this-worldly and other-worldly. There is a fine line of continuity within the transformation that is implicit in the promise of a new creation in the light of the bodily resurrection of Jesus from the dead.

When we turn to nature, which is our primary concern here, we discover that nature itself is full of promise. John F. Haught, more imaginatively than most, has opened new vistas for understanding what might be involved in the promise of a new creation. According to Haught, nature is 'seeded with promise' and 'pregnant with a mysterious future'.[17]

It is clear that nature, human nature and non-human nature, is not yet complete and remains an unfinished symphony and an unfinished work of art. It is this incomplete character of the world we live in that inspires, as Denise Levertov does at the beginning of this chapter, a promise with hope for the fullness of life and a new communion. In this regard, Haught talks about 'the lavish and gratuitous profusion' of the natural world as 'an instalment of the extravagant future fulfilment towards which faith perceives all of life and the whole cosmic story to be summoned by God'.[18]

d. The Link between 'Creation out of Nothing' and Prayer

The importance of this theology of creation, especially in relation to creation out of nothing, continuous creation and the new creation, is that it captures, however inadequately, a little of the character of the God who is the 'object' of the praise of nature and creatures: love, unity, sovereignty, graciousness, relationality, creativity, fidelity, empowerment and the unfailing presence of God to creation as both origin and goal of life. In describing God in these terms, we must remember as always that we speak in metaphorical, symbolic and analogical terms. There comes a moment when the dynamism of prayer and worship invites us to go beyond human constructs. This awareness of the limitation of all language surrounding God facilitates what some call a mystical moment within prayer and worship. The immanence of God in prayer and worship is incomplete unless it brings us from time to time into the dazzling darkness of God's transcendence. The God who creates out of nothing continues to hold creation together, and promises to fulfil the ongoing gift of creation in the fullness of time, described in different ways, such as the new creation in Christ, or the new heaven and the new earth. It is in

17. John F. Haught, *The Promise of Nature: Ecology and Cosmic Purpose*, New York, NY: Paulist Press, 1993, 109–10.
18. John F. Haught, 'Response from John F. Haught', in *Ecotheology: A Christian Conversation*, edited by Kiara A. Jorgenson and Alan G. Padgett, Grand Rapids, MI: W. B. Eerdmans Publishing Company, 2021, 164.

virtue of the Christ-event that we can see the unity of creation in terms of beginnings and endings. The God who initiates, the Creator Spirit of God, is the same Spirit who will complete all things in Christ.

In effect, the world inhabited by the biblical authors, especially in the Psalms, Isaiah and Job, is a theocentric world, and not the anthropocentric universe of so much modern thinking. It is only in virtue of living in a theocentric world or, better, a pneumato-centric universe, that it is possible to understand what it might mean for nature to praise God. Some agree, as seen in Chapter 2, that nature praising God is an antidote to anthropocentrism (Bauckham) and a rebuke of humanity's self-absorption (Horrell). Nature has value in itself, and is not something external to the creation of humanity, nor is it intended simply to serve the needs of human beings. It is salutary to remember that nature preceded the advent of *Homo sapiens* and that nature by being itself praised God before humans did. The different texts around nature praising God suggest, as seen in Chapter 2, that nature in itself praises God and that this praise is not dependent on humans. Many of the texts in the Psalms and elsewhere are liturgical in tone, and others are eschatological in orientation. As eschatological, these texts are a reminder that the liturgy should embody an eschatological perspective and, as such, point the world beyond its introverted self.[19] The different nature-praising texts in the Bible cannot be dismissed as merely poetic in a pejorative sense, without calling into question the meaning and content of all religious language. These nature-praising texts capture and recover the power of beauty within liturgy. This beauty of nature needs to be incorporated visibly into the different liturgies conducted by human beings. This could be done, not only by having parts of nature present in the liturgy, but also by incorporating the symphonic sounds of nature into the liturgy, especially the polyphonic sounds of birds and animals in both their groaning and their praising of the Creator. Nature has value in itself and has its own graced integrity and is not, therefore, available simply to serve the needs of human beings. This value and integrity of nature evokes a sense of awe and wonder.

---

19. See Dermot A. Lane, 'Eucharist as Sacrament of the *Eschaton*: A Failure of the Imagination?', in *50th International Eucharistic Congress: Proceedings of the International Symposium of Theology*, Dublin: Veritas Publications, 2013, 399–414.

Nature is alive with creativity, diversity and beauty, which have become more evident than ever before through the findings of contemporary science. Nature is radically relational internally and externally, which makes her open to the possibility of new relationships beyond herself, just as human beings are open to new relationships beyond themselves, precisely because both nature and humanity have been graced by the same creative Spirit of God and continue to be graced by that Spirit, as seen in Chapter 4.

It is helpful to see nature as a book to be read, a text to be interpreted, a voice to be heard, and the bearer of pneumatological presence to be celebrated with gratitude in our liturgies. As a book and as a voice, nature is capable of giving praise to the Creator, enriching and expanding the horizons of Christian liturgy.

In other words, nature praising God, as found in the Bible, requires theological support to be meaningful in the twenty-first century, especially if it is to have an impact on the liturgy of the Christian churches. One important theological support is an understanding of the world as the household (*oikos*) of God, or, as Pope Francis says in his encyclical, 'our common home', or, as tradition says, 'the sacrament of God's presence' in the world. In saying this, we must move beyond pantheism or deism into a panentheism that opens up the way for 'seeing' the eternal Word of God personally embodied in the flesh of Jesus of Nazareth. This sacramental view of the universe is, as seen in Chapter 4, based first of all on the unity of a theology of creation and the doctrine of Deep Incarnation. The theology of creation is multi-layered. It should include at least, as already seen, reference to creation out of nothing, the ongoing gift of creation, and the promise of a new creation. Above all else, nature must be reincorporated and reintegrated into the body of creation itself if we are to see it praising God, and if all creatures, human and non-human, are to join together in giving greater glory to God. At the centre of this foundational theology of the natural world is the notion of creation as gift. Without an appreciation of creation as gift, and without an experience of the beauty of creation, there will be no feeling of gratitude and no sense of thankfulness. It is the experience of creation as gift and the bearer of beauty that leads to the praise of God.

Liturgy at present is in need of reform, a reform that began at the Second Vatican Council (1962–65) and remains unfinished to this day. For this recommendation of reform to be accepted, we need to remind ourselves of the importance of the principle of inculturation that requires a recognition of the dynamic relationship that exists between faith and culture, worship and community, religion and science.

According to Thomas Reese, one of the greatest challenges facing the churches in the twenty-first century is how to celebrate the liturgy in a way that takes account of the beauty of God's creation made manifest by contemporary science. For Reese, our current 'liturgical worship requires that we park our scientific minds at the church door and enter into the prescientific world of our ancestors when we pray'.[20] Is it not possible in this digital era of the creative arts to combine the liturgical wisdom of the past with the insights of contemporary culture?

Another way of spelling out the meaning of Nature Praising God is to suggest that the 'who' of liturgy is not simply human beings, but the whole living community of creation. This thesis about creation's praise of God is only sustainable on a number of assumptions scattered throughout this book. These include that it is in virtue of the origins of creation 'in the beginning' by the creative breath of God that it is possible for creation to praise God Further, it is also based on the assumption of eschatological destiny of creation in Christ. More particularly, it is in view of the fact that every particular part of creation fulfils a specific role within the greater scheme of things by being itself. It is in fulfilling that role that nature praises God. And, it is in virtue of God's continuous act of creation of holding everything together that creation can be said to praise God.

In teasing out the significance of nature praising God it is important to highlight what this does not mean. Creation's praise of God is not about adding creation as a theme to the liturgy. Nor is it about giving thanks to God for the gift of creation. Nor is it about making creation more visible within the liturgy, even though each of these objectives is

---

20. Thomas Reese, '*Eucharistic* prayer in the 21st century', in *National Catholic Reporter*, 12 January 2017.

important in itself. Instead, there is something more radical been proposed here, namely that it is the whole living community of creation that gives glory to God the creator, and not just human beings.[21]

As Pope Francis points out in *Laudato Si'*: 'When we see God reflected in all that exists, our hearts are moved… to worship him in union with them' (87). Towards the end of the encyclical he reminds us that in the Eucharist 'the whole Cosmos gives thanks to God' (236).[22]

It is in the light of these different aspects of the theology of creation, however inadequately expressed here, that we can conclude that nature praising God begins to make sense spiritually, liturgically, theologically and eschatologically. For this to happen a culture of care and gratitude must replace the contemporary culture of profit.[23] As such, the much-neglected presence of creation praising God in the natural world has power to renew, reform and deepen our understanding of Christian liturgy in the twenty-first century.

21. This way of explaining nature's praise of God is spelt out persuasively in an original article by Teresa Burger, 'All you have created rightly gives you praise: Rethinking liturgical studies, Re-rooting worship in creation' in *Ex Fonte-Journal of Ecumenical Studies and Liturgy* 1 (2022) 5–20.
22. This quotation is developed further in Dermot Lane, *Theology and Ecology in Dialogue*, 138–146.
23. The importance of promoting a culture of care and gratitude is a key theme running through Archbishop Dermot Farrell's pastoral letter entitled *The Cry of the Earth – The Cry of the Poor*, Dublin: Veritas, 2021, pages 18–19 and 34–37.

EPILOGUE

Gathering Up the Fragments: Towards a Theology of Creation Praising God

THIS SMALL book began by trying to retrieve a forgotten tradition in the Bible about nature praising God. To the ears of the modern world, the idea of nature praising God sounds alien and even unintelligible because nature is all too often regarded as inert and lifeless. To the ears of others, it sounded like one of those biblical insights that might have something to say to the much-needed reform of Christian worship in the twenty-first century.

With that in mind we explored a sample of texts in the Bible that talk explicitly about nature praising God. We examined the views of scripture scholars and theologians on the possible meanings of these texts. It became clear that one of the obstacles to understanding nature praising God is the dominance of an anthropocentric and instrumentalist view of nature. What is needed to overcome this human-centred view of nature is a non-anthropocentric theology of nature. It becomes possible to move towards a non-anthropocentric theology of nature by moving from the domination model of creation to a community model of creation. Creation is a living community of all God's creatures, each of which has a role to play in a universe that is radically interrelational, interdependent and interconnected. In support of this shift, we began to see nature as a graced-endowed reality, charged with the grandeur of God, a book to be read and, as such, having a sacramental feeling to it.

More specifically in support of a non-anthropocentric theology of nature, we examined what light pneumatology and Christology could shed on the possibility of a non-anthropocentric view of nature. Pneumatology points to the universal presence of the gift of the Spirit poured out on the world 'in the beginning'. This Spirit of God pervades the whole of creation from the beginning and this enables us to see the whole of nature as teeming with life and creativity.

A nature-based Christology revealed that the renewal of the natural world is envisaged as part of the coming reign of God. Equally important, we discovered that the emerging doctrine of Deep Incarnation has important things to say about the sacred character of the natural world. A nature-based Christology, especially one that focuses on Deep Incarnation, reveals fundamental 'qualities' about nature that are pertinent to making sense of nature praising God.

The book closes with an outline of different dimensions to creation, which include creation out of nothing, the ongoing gift of continuous creation and the promise of a new creation, and a new heaven and a new earth, in Christ. For many, the theology of creation out of nothing has become marginal to faith. Yet we discovered that creation out of nothing is of profound significance for Christian prayer and worship, and contains important 'implications' for grasping the meaning of nature praising God.

In the light of this simplified overview, it is time to summarise some of the forgotten 'qualities' of nature and to outline some of the 'implications' of nature praising God for Christian liturgy in the twenty-first century.

1. The *Qualities* of Nature as a Subject
Deep Incarnation calls for a recovery of:

- The *integrity* of the natural world;
- The intrinsic *value* of nature in itself, in the sight of humanity, and the sight of the Creator;
- The *sacred character* of the natural world;
- A new locus for appreciating the *meaning of the cosmic Christ* in Pauline texts;

- A *new respect* for the natural world in itself;
- A basis for developing an *incarnational theology of nature*, that is a theology that perceives the presence of God permeating the life of the natural world;
- A challenge for *humanity to reconsider its place* in the natural world;
- The *interdependence* of all God's creatures in nature;
- The *dignity* of the natural world;
- The presence in varying degrees of some form of *interiority/subjectivity/consciousness/agency within the natural world.*

2. The *Implications* of Nature as a Subject Praising God

In a similar way we need to outline some of the 'implications' of nature praising God for liturgy in the twenty-first century.

Nature praising God:

- is a corrective to an excessive and exclusive anthropo-centric view of liturgy. The praise of God is not exclusive to humans; it can be found in varying degrees in the life and creativity of nature itself;
- stands out as a rebuke of humanity's egocentric self-absorption at the expense of other creatures in the universe;
- is not something dependent on humanity. Instead, we saw that for many, nature praises God by being itself and contributing whatever it has to offer to the wider web of life within the greater plan of the Creator;
- is salutary reminder that nature's praise of God pre-cedes humanity's praise of God and, as such, has influenced the shape and character of the worship of God by humans;
- challenges humanity to join the cosmic choir in giving glory to God. The liturgy of the cosmos, especially in the Psalms, and the liturgy of the Christian community have become overly separated and isolated from each other;

- is a call for some form of mutuality between the liturgy of the natural world and the liturgy of the Christian community in giving thanks and praise to God jointly;
- is a summons to include the sounds of nature, in their praise and lament, as part of the liturgy of the Christian church;
- is a call to embrace more fully the shape, colours and beauty of nature in a way that enriches the quality of Christian liturgy;
- is an invitation to humanity to enter into a universal communion with the whole of creation in giving thanks and honour and glory to the Creator.

These different 'qualities' of nature and 'implications' of nature praising God provide the ingredients of a new story about the natural world for the twenty-first century that can enrich an understanding of humanity's place in the world and the quality of Christian liturgy for this century.

Appendices

1. St Francis of Assisi (1181/82–1226), 'The Canticle of Creation'

O Most High, all-powerful, good Lord God,
to you belong praise, glory,
honour and all blessing.
Be praised, my Lord, for all your creation
and especially for our Brother Sun,
who brings us the day and the light;
he is strong and shines magnificently.
O Lord, we think of you when we look at him.
Be praised, my Lord, for Sister Moon,
and for the stars
which you have set shining and lovely
in the heavens.
Be praised, my Lord,
for our Brothers Wind and Air
and every kind of weather
by which you, Lord,
uphold life in all your creatures.
Be praised, my Lord, for Sister Water,
who is very useful to us,
and humble and precious and pure.
Be praised, my Lord, for Brother Fire,
through whom you give us light in the darkness:
he is bright and lively and strong.
Be praised, my Lord,
for Sister Earth, our Mother,
who nourishes us and sustains us,
bringing forth
fruits and vegetables of many kinds
and flowers of many colours.
Be praised, my Lord,
for those who forgive for love of you;

and for those
who bear sickness and weakness
in peace and patience
– you will grant them a crown.
Be praised, my Lord, for our Sister Death,
whom we must all face.
I praise and bless you, Lord,
and I give thanks to you,
and I will serve you in all humility.

2. Pope Francis, 'A Christian Prayer in Union with Creation'

Father, we praise you with all your creatures.
They came forth from your all-powerful hand;
they are yours, filled with your presence and your tender love.
Praise be to you!

Son of God, Jesus,
through you all things were made.
You were formed in the womb of Mary our Mother,
you became part of this earth,
and you gazed upon this world with human eyes.
Today you are alive in every creature in your risen glory.
Praise be to you!

Holy Spirit, by your light
you guide this world towards the Father's love
and accompany creation as it groans in travail.
You also dwell in our hearts
and you inspire us to do what is good.
Praise be to you!

Triune Lord, wondrous community of infinite love,
teach us to contemplate you
in the beauty of the universe,
for all things speak of you.
Awaken our praise and thankfulness

for every being that you have made.
Give us the grace to feel profoundly joined
to everything that is.

God of love, show us our place in this world
as channels of your
love for all the creatures of this earth,
for not one of them is forgotten in your sight.
Enlighten those who possess power and money
that they may avoid the sin of indifference,
that they may love the common good, advance the weak,
and care for this world in which we live.
The poor and the earth are crying out.
O Lord, seize us with your power and light,
help us to protect all life,
to prepare for a better future,
for the coming of your Kingdom
of justice, peace, love and beauty.
Praise be to you!

Amen.

Select Bibliography

Bauckham, Richard, *The Bible and Ecology: Rediscovering the Community of Creation*, London: Darton, Longman & Todd, 2010.

Bergant, Dianne, *A New Heaven, A New Earth: The Bible and Catholicity*, New York, NY: Orbis Books, 2016.

Berger, Theresa (ed.), *Full of your Glory: Liturgy, Cosmos, Creation*, Collegeville, MN: Liturgical Press, 2019.

Brown, William P., *The Seven Pillars of Creation: The Bible, Science and the Ecology of Wonder*, Oxford: Oxford University Press, 2010.

Carrol, Denis, *Towards a Story of the Earth: Essays in the theology of Creation*, Dublin: Dominican Publications, 1987.

Castelo, Daniel, *Pneumatology: A Guide for the Perplexed*, New York, NY: Bloomsbury T&T Clark, 2015.

Conradie, Ernst M., Bergmann, Sigurd, Deane-Drummond Celia, and Edwards Denis (eds.), *Christian Faith and the Earth: Current Paths and Emerging Horizons in Eco-Theology*, New York, NY: Bloomsbury T&T Clark, 2014

Daly Denton, Margaret, *John: An Earth Bible Commentary: Supposing Him to Be the Gardener*, London: Bloomsbury T&T Clark, 2017.

Delio, Ilia (ed.), *From Teilhard to Omega: Co-creating an Unfinished Universe*, New York, NY: Orbis Books, 2014.

Delio, Ilia (ed.), *Making All Things New: Catholicity, Cosmology, Consciousness*, New York, NY: Orbis Books, 2015.

DiLeo, Dan (ed.), *All Creation is Connected: Voices in Response to Pope Francis's Encyclical on Ecology*, Winona, MN: Anselm Academic, 2018.

Edwards, Denis (ed.), *Earth Revealing – Earth Healing: Ecology and Christian Theology*, Collegeville, MN: Liturgical Press, 2001.

Edwards, Denis, *Ecology at the Heart of Faith: The Change of Heart that Leads to a New Way of Living on Earth*, New York, NY: Orbis Books, 2006.

Edwards, Denis, *How God Acts: Creation, Redemption, and Special Divine Action*, Minneapolis, MN: Fortress Press, 2010.

Edwards, Denis, *Christian Understandings of Creation: The Historical Trajectory*, Minneapolis, MN: Fortress Press, 2017.

Edwards, Denis, *The Natural World and God: Theological Explorations*, Adelaide: ATF Press, 2017.

Edwards, Denis, *Deep Incarnation: God's Redemptive Suffering with Creatures*, New York, NY: Orbis Books, 2019.

Farrell, Dermot, Archbishop of Dublin, *The Cry of the Earth – the Cry of the Poor*, A Pastoral Letter, Dublin: Veritas Publications, 2021.

Feehan, John, *Every Bush a Flame: Science, God and the Natural World*, Dublin: Veritas Publications, 2021.

Fretheim, Terence E., *God and the World in the Old Testament: A Relational Theology of Creation*, Nashville, TN: Abington Press, 2005.

Ghosh, Amitav, *The Nutmeg's Curse: Parables for a Planet in Crisis*, Chicago, IL: The University of Chicago Press, 2021.

Gold, Lorna, *Climate Generation: Awakening to our Children's Future*, Dublin: Veritas Publications, 2018.

Gregersen, Niels Henrik (ed.), *Incarnation: On the Scope and Depth of Christology*, Philadelphia, PA: Fortress Press, 2013.

Haught, John F., *The Promise of Nature: Ecology and Cosmic Purpose*, Mahwah, NJ: Paulist Press, 1993.

Haught, John F., *Resting on the Future: Catholic Theology for an Unfinished Universe*, New York, NY: Bloomsbury, 2015.

Haught, John F., *The New Cosmic Story: Inside our Awakening Universe*, New Haven, CT: Yale University Press, 2017.

Horan, Daniel P., *All God's Creatures: A Theology of Creation*, New York, NY: Lexington Books/ Fortress Academic, 2018.

Johnson, Elizabeth A., *Women, Earth, and Creator Spirit*, The 1993 Madeleva Lecture in Spirituality, Mahwah, NJ: Paulist Press, 1993.

Johnson, Elizabeth A., *Ask the Beasts: Darwin and the God of Love*, New York, NY: Bloomsbury Continuum, 2014.

Johnson, Elizabeth A., *Abounding in Kindness: Writings for the People of God*, New York, NY: Orbis Books, 2015.

Johnson, Elizabeth A., *Creation and the Cross: The Mercy of God for a Planet in Peril*, New York, NY: Orbis Books, 2018.

Kelly, Anthony J., *Integral Ecology and the Fullness of Life: Theological and Philosophical Perspectives*, Mahwah, NJ: Paulist Press, 2018.

Klein, Naomi, *On Fire: The Burning Case for a Green New Deal*, London: Allen Lane, an imprint of Penguin books, 2019.

Kureethadam, Joshtrum, *Creation in Crisis: Science, Ethics, Theology*, New York: Orbis Books, 2014

Lennan, Richard, and Pineda-Madrid Nancy, (eds.), *The Holy Spirit: Setting the World on Fire*, Mahwah, NJ: Paulist Press, 2017.

McDonagh, Seán, *To Care for the Earth: A Call to a New Theology*, London: Chapman, 1986.

McDonagh, Seán, *On Care for our Common Home, Laudato Si': the Encyclical of Pope Francis on the Environment, with comments by Seán McDonagh*, New York, NY: Orbis Books, 2016.

McDonagh, Seán (ed.), *Laudato Si', An Irish Response: Essays on the Pope's Letter on the Environment*, Dublin: Veritas Publications, 2017.

McKim, Robert, *Laudato Si' and the Environment: Pope Francis's Green Encyclical*, London: Routledge, 2020.

Mickey, Sam, Kelly, Seán, and Robert, Adam (eds.), *The Variety of Integral Ecologies: Nature, Culture, and Knowledge in the Planetary Era*, New York, NY: SUNY Press, 2017.

Miller, Vincent J. (ed.), *The Theological and Ecological Vision of Laudato Si': Everything is Connected*, New York, NY: Bloomsbury T&T Clark, 2017.

Northcott, Michael S., and Scott, Peter M., (eds.), *Systematic Theology and Climate Change: Ecumenical Perspectives*, London: Routledge, 2014.

Oliver, Simon, *Creation: A Guide for the Perplexed*, London: Bloomsbury, 2017.

Robinson, Mary, *Climate Justice: Hope, Resilience and the Fight for a Sustainable Future*, London: Bloomsbury, 2018.

Robinson, Mary, *Climate Justice: A Man-made Problem with a Feminist Solution*, London: Bloomsbury Publishing, 2018

Russell, Robert J., *Cosmology, Evolution and Resurrection Hope: Theology and Science in Creative Mutual Interaction*, Ontario: Pandora Press, 2006.

Sheid, Daniel P., *The Cosmic Common Good: Religious Grounds for Ecological Ethics*, New York, NY: Oxford University Press, 2016.

Teilhard de Chardin, Pierre, *Hymn of the Universe*, London: Collins, 1965.

Thunberg, Greta, *No One Is Too Small to Make a Difference*, London: Penguin Books, 2019.

Tilley, Terrence, W., *The Disciples' Jesus: Christology as Reconciling Practice*, New York, NY: Orbis Books, 2008.

Tucker, Mary Evelyn (ed.), *Thomas Berry, The Sacred Universe: Earth, Spirituality and Religion in the 21st Century*, with a Foreword by Mary Evelyn Tucker, New York, NY: Columbia University Press, 2009.

Tucker, Mary Evelyn and Grimm, John, (eds.), *Living Cosmology: Christian Responses to Journey of the Universe*, New York, NY: Orbis Books, 2016.

Tucker, Mary Evelyn, Grimm, John, and Angyal, Andrew, *Thomas Berry: A Biography*, New York, NY: Columbia University Press, 2019.

Vince, Catherine, *Worship and the new Cosmology: Liturgical and Theological Challenges*, Collegeville, MN: Liturgical Press, 2014.

Quotations from the Second Vatican Council documents are taken from *Vatican Council II: Constitutions, Decrees, Declarations*, ed. by Austin Flannery, OP, a completely revised translation in inclusive language, Dublin: Dominican Publications, 1996.

Biblical quotations are taken from the New Revised Standard Version Bible, New York: Oxford University Press, 1991, unless otherwise stated.

Index

121